Pick-Up Lines That Work

Pick-Up Lines That Work

Get the Girl Tonight!

by Devon 'Mack' Wild

iUniverse, Inc.
New York Lincoln Shanghai

Pick-Up Lines That Work
Get the Girl Tonight!

iUniverse, Inc.

For information address:
iUniverse, Inc.
2021 Pine Lake Road, Suite 100
Lincoln, NE 68512
www.iuniverse.com

ISBN: 0-595-32368-5

Printed in the United States of America

Contents

Foreword

Women are one of life's greatest pleasures. Meeting a beautiful woman and attracting her interest is an experience like nothing else. However, the problem for a lot of men is that they don't know how to approach a woman or even know what to say to her.

I experienced that same problem shortly after I graduated from college when the plethora of women available on college campus and fraternity parties were no longer available. Night after night I witnessed guys who were less attractive than myself winning the girls over. What did they have that I didn't have?

I read books on picking up women but none seemed to provide an easy-to-follow formula for doing so. I decided to befriend some of the masters and learn first hand what these average looking guys did to win the girls over. It was through this experience that I came up with the flawless PJCSP pick-up formula. Using this pick-up formula I have now picked up more woman from the bar scene than I could have ever imagined.

I have put this elusive information into my new book *Pick-Up Lines That Work: Get the Girl Tonight!* With over 1500 pick-up lines at your disposal, you'll never be dumbfounded again upon seeing the woman of your dreams. The pick-up lines contain certain chick-magnet elements that will separate you from the other guys using ineffective pick-up lines. This competitive advantage will give you the confidence and edge over the competition.

If you study these pick-up lines and the flawless PJCSP pick-up formula you'll learn a system that makes picking up women easy. Enjoy your life and start winning with girls.

Enjoy,

Devon "Mack" Wild

Chapter 1
How To Use
Pick-Up Lines That Work

Pick-Up Lines That Work can be read straight through or on an as needed basis. It has sixteen chapters covering the most common places to pick up on women including the bar, car, gym, coffee shop, dance club, video store, Internet, grocery store, mall, parties, and more.

There are multiple pick-up lines for each environment so you can find the one or ones that fit you, the girl, and/or the situation just perfectly. The tone of the pick-up lines range from humorous, to complimentary, to ridiculous, to sexual. The pick-up line that you choose will depend on the type of relationship you're seeking.

If you are seeking a one-night stand then you are going to use the more aggressive/sexual pick-up lines or you might even dip into Chapter 14 to utilize Rude And Crude Pick-Up Lines. If you are more interested in dating or a relationship then you will probably want to use the pick-up lines that are more humorous or complimentary. The choice is up to you.

Each chapter begins with a short introduction to the specific women-meeting environment. The introduction is followed by at least eighty pick-up lines specifically tailored to that particular environment. However, to be the most successful in your pursuit of women, I recommend you follow the flawless pick-up formula called PJCSP.

PJCSP

PJCSP is an acronym for **p**ick-up line, **j**oke, **c**ompliment, **s**mall talk, and **p**hone number. This pick-up formula was developed through conversations, observations, and experiences with some of the best pick-up artists in the United States. Using PJCSP you separate yourself from the competition by marking yourself as a consummate ladies man. While your competition is stumbling for words you'll have every girl's devout attention with a grabbing pick-up line for attention, joke for a laugh, compliment for endearment, small talk for sincerity, and her phone number for the reward.

The flawless PJCSP pick-up formula is no gimmick. It is a system built on basic human psychology. Women are attracted to men for many reasons but a major one is how men make them feel. Women and human beings in general like to laugh, like to receive compliments, like to be listened to and the PJCSP method is based on these truths. This five-step formula gives every bachelor, whether handsome or heinous, a proven and easy way to pick up more women more often.

Pick-Up Line: the First "P" of PJCSP

This book primarily focuses on the pick-up line, which is the first and foremost element of PJCSP. The pick-up line is of integral importance because it sets the girl's first impression, establishes the mood, and it gives her that first glimpse into who you are. Commonly a guy will approach a girl and say "what's up," "what's your name," or "what's going on?" These are the rote come-ons that girls have heard a million times.

Most pick-up lines don't work because they are trite, cheesy, and closed-ended statements. Others don't work because of their overt sexual overtones. The pick-up lines that do work tend to follow certain rules.

The best pick-up lines follow three important rules:

1. The pick-up line should be in the form of a question.

    Most pick-up lines are just stale closed-ended statements. Take for instance the pick-up line: "Baby I'm no Fred Flinstone, but I can make your Bed-rock." This type of statement pick-up line doesn't make it easy for a girl to respond. When a pick-up line is in the form of a question it fosters conversation.

For example, if you take a pick-up line from *Pick-Up Lines That Work* such as "Do you think I look more like Forest Gump or Rain Man?" you make it very easy for the girl to engage in conversation.

2.   The pick-up line should be humorous and tasteful.

You want the girl to laugh or smile, not to slap you in the face. Take for instance the pick-up line: "Why don't you sit in my lap and we'll talk about whatever pops up first." This type of sex-based pick-up line might make your buddies chuckle but the girl will most likely be offended and take you for a pervert.

On the other hand if you take a pick-up line from *Pick-Up Lines That Work* such as "Do I look fat in these jeans?" your humor will be welcomed. You will always win using pick-up lines that are humorous and tasteful.

3.   The pick-up line should be original.

No one likes to hear the same joke twice and the same goes for pick-up lines. If you've heard the line before then it's best to choose a different one.

The majority of the pick-up lines in this book observe these three rules. You'll find yourself much more successful when using pick-up lines that follow these rules.

Delivery of the Pick-Up Line

No matter what type of relationship you are seeking, the delivery of the pick-up line is crucial. Reading these pick-up lines on your couch in not going to be good enough. You must put yourself in front of a mirror and practice, practice, practice.

Your body language is almost more important than the pick-up line itself. Many communication experts agree that what you say in a face-to-face interaction only counts for twenty percent of the perceived message. What this means is that the girl will be paying great attention to your face expression, posture, energy level, and tone of voice. On this note, if you deliver a great pick-up line with a static face expression you're not likely to get far. However, if you deliver a pick-up line with a smile that radiates confidence, she might be making you breakfast tomorrow morning.

When you visualize picking up a woman, think about the bar scene in the movie "Top Gun" when Maverick (Tom Cruise) courts Charlie (Kelly McGillis) by singing "You've Lost That Loving Feeling." He does it with confidence, charisma, and a smile. That is how you want to deliver your pick-up line, however you can save the singing part for the shower.

Go to your bathroom mirror and take a look at yourself. Stand up straight, take your hands out of your pockets, and put on your seductive-but-friendly gaze. Now with a smile, practice a few pick-up lines from Chapter 2: Anytime Pick-Up Lines.

As you practice, focus on your smile. Everyone loves a great smile. A smile disarms a woman. It tells her that you come in peace. Tom Cruise and Julia Roberts didn't climb to the top of their game because of their frowns. Now your smile may not be a million bucks but whose is. Don't forget, Tom Cruise is short and has a big nose. He's not perfect and he sure doesn't let those shortcomings get in his way.

The pick-up line is a great way to start the conversation, but a successful pick up must continue with more positive emotional arousal. A joke is the best way to continue your interaction with the lady.

Joke: The "J" of PJCSP

The joke is the second step in the PJCSP pick-up formula. Many men fail in approaching women because their approach is too serious and dry. A joke is a great way to show her that you have a sense of humor and you're fun to be around.

Don't ask her permission to tell her the joke, just jump right into it. Always assume she's interested in you and what you have to say. Your confidence will captivate her.

The goal of the joke is to put a smile on her face. A smile is tangible evidence that you are able to evoke positive emotion from her. Throughout the PJCSP pick-up formula you will continue to evoke positive emotion. Once you see the smile on her face you are that much closer to a phone number.

If you know some great jokes then you're set. If not, check out one of these great websites:

- www.jokes.com—This site has a great assortment of jokes and lists them by categories including: sexuality, gross, yo mama, blonde, zombie baby, waspy to your mama, office, politics, bar, redneck, and lawyer.

- www.funny.com—This site has a jokes section which includes a "Top Current Joke" section which contains jokes that people have rated as the funniest jokes.

- www.jokingaround.com—This site has a rating system for their jokes with G, PG, and PG-13. The jokes here are clean and quite funny and would be the perfect type of jokes for a woman that you are interested in dating and/or building a relationship with.

Once you have her laughing, it's time to pay her a specific compliment.

Compliment: the "C" of PJCSP

The compliment is the third step in PJCSP. Every woman loves a compliment. Attractive women are used to hearing compliments on a daily basis. You can better your competition by making your compliment specific. The more specific the better. Being specific always wins more points with a woman. For example:

- "I love your contagious laugh."

- "Your perfume is extraordinary or is that your natural scent?"

- "Your eyes sparkle like diamonds."

- "I thought Julia Roberts had a great smile."

- "I love your long delicate fingers."

Remember, you are trying to separate yourself from the slew of other men out there. Make your compliment original and you will win points.

Small Talk: the "S" of PJCSP

Small talk is the fourth step in PJCSP. Small talk is to show her your sincere side. Introduce yourself. Ask her where she's from, her favorite color, her favorite TV show, what she eats for breakfast, or any other somewhat interesting question that you can think of. This is the time to show her that you can listen.

Most men are too buy talking about themselves to listen. This is where you can gain an edge over your competition. A man that can listen is a rare breed. If you show a woman that you're a good listener she'll find you irresistible. Listen, smile, and laugh if appropriate.

Phone Number: the Last "P" of PJCSP

Getting the girl's phone number is the last step of PJCSP. Don't bore the girl to death with the mundane chores that you do during the day. After you enchanted her with your pick-up line, amused her with a joke, endeared yourself to her with your specific compliment, and exchanged a little small talk for sincerity, then the phone number is in order.

The idea here is to excite her emotions and then leave her wanting more. It's the simple law of supply and demand. When there's less supply there's more demand. Elvis Presley's manager applied this principle to his live performances and it worked marvelously. He performed less shows than other musicians, but his shows were always an event. Always leave the girl wanting more.

So how and when do you make your exit? At some point when your small talk with the lady is going great, take a quick peak at your watch. At that point you need to give her a great excuse to leave. The exit script below always works great.

- "Shoot! I was supposed to meet my friend down at Dublin's (Insert your local bar here) five minutes ago. You're amazing! Let me get your phone number so I can hear that engaging laugh again."

Once you get her digits it's time to go to the next bar and start all over. It's that simple.

It's All About the Numbers

Even though you're armed with the best pick-up lines on the market, you can't win every girl one-hundred percent of the time. It's important that you note your results and move right on to the next girl until you are able to fulfill the entire

PJCSP cycle. The most important thing to remember when picking up women is to persevere through the face of rejection.

Too many men get caught up in the face of rejection. You have to get used to rejection in picking up women or you'll never achieve the level where you want to be. Remember, many girls who go out have boyfriends or husbands. Many girls are lesbians or are psychologically disturbed. There are many other reasons why even if you deliver the best game in the world you're not going to pick them up. This is why it is so crucial that you move on to the next girl right after a defeat.

Rest assured that you'll get many smiles, laughs, phone numbers, and dates with *Pick-Up Lines That Work*. However, you must adopt a style of unbreakable confidence. There is a great line in the teen-sex comedy movie "Fast Times At Ridgemont High" when the character Damone tells his virgin-buddy Rat a pick-up maxim: "The attitude dictates that you don't care if she comes, stays, lays, or prays. No matter what happens, your toes are still tapping." Once you put your emotions into the game you're done.

Get Yourself a Wingman

If you really want to succeed with *Pick-Up Lines That Work* and its dogma, you'll need to get yourself a wingman. By wingman I mean a friend that has the same passion for picking up women as yourself. The reasons to have a wingman are many.

First, the support. Anything awesome that was ever accomplished wasn't done so without great effort. And when great effort is involved it's wonderful to have support. Your wingman can console you when you strike out and rejoice with you when you succeed.

Second, the positive imagery. If a man has a friend or friends, a woman sees that he social. Not that if you're alone that it's necessarily a bad thing, but it puts a woman a little on the defensive.

Third, someone to keep her friend busy. If the girl that you're talking to has a friend you're going to need a wingman to keep her busy. If you fail to occupy her friend, her friend will grow jealous and will try to take the girl away from you and move to another location where there is two guys. Her friend might also say negative things about you in her jealous rage.

If you are going to make an attempt to pick up on a girl with a friend you need to make sure you maintain eye contact with both of them and toss a compliment to her friend also. The moral of the story is: Get a wingman!

If you're out solo there are many things you can say to make it look like you have a friend with you. You can say such things as:

- "My buddy is in the back talking to some girl."
- "My buddy took off with a girl."
- "My buddy hasn't showed up yet."

A woman would generally prefer these responses rather than:

- "I'm just here hanging with myself."

WARNING: It's better to roll solo than to go out with a bunch of guys who just sit around, drink beer, and look at the girls but don't do anything. I'm not saying to diss your good buddies, but if you want to meet girls you're going to have to make some changes. You want to have a wingman or wingmen who have the same mission and brass balls as yourself.

Now obviously there are going to be times when you're not with your wingman/ wingmen (like when you're walking, driving, at the gym) but hopefully with all the practice that you've had with him/them you won't even need that support.

Track Your Results

For best results and to get the most use out of *Pick-Up Lines That Work* you should keep a journal of your nights out. Keep track of which pick-up lines seem to work for you and other bits of the interactions that really seemed to go well.

A little pocket notebook is great but a palm pilot is even better. Take notes and keep a log at home in an Excel or another similar worksheet file. Remember, any greatness that was ever achieved was not done so without hard work.

Get to Work

Rome wasn't built in a day, but with *Pick-Up Lines That Work* you are now armed to meet more women with more success than you've ever had before. Practice makes perfect. Use *Pick-Up Lines That Work* tonight!

Chapter 2
Anytime Pick-Up Lines

Anytime Pick-Up Lines are great because they can be used in all environments and situations. These lines can be used anywhere anytime, whether you're at the post office or McDonald's. With over two hundred Anytime Pick-Up Lines you don't have any excuses not to be picking up on women 24-7-365. Go get them!

1. Do you think I look more like Tom Cruise or Brad Pitt?

   • Obviously you probably look like neither but that's the funny part. You can follow it up if she hesitates with: "Seriously!".

2. Don't hate me because I'm beautiful.

   • A woman finds this funny because men are considered handsome not beautiful. It's even more humorous if you're not particularly beautiful.

3. Do I remind you more of Forest Gump or Rain Man?

   • Women like confident men and using self-effacing humor such as this lets a woman know that you can poke a little fun at yourself.

4. I was working the other day and this girl outside kept on staring at me. Was that you?

   • This puts the power into your court because the girl was staring at you and you're just following up on it. When she says "no" just follow up with: "Well she looked just like you."

5. Are you falling in love with me?

   • Proposing such a preposterous question to a stranger always gets a laugh.

6. I've been working out. Can you tell?

    - This is best used for a man that has a nice beer gut because of its ironic nature.
    - If you do have a nice body then it's not as funny but it gives the girl a reason to check you out without feeling guilty.

7. It's my birthday!

    - A great way to begin the conversation because almost anybody with a heart is going to tell you "Happy Birthday" and give you a smile and a hug if you're lucky.

8. Do you want to get married?

    - Proposing such a preposterous question on a stranger always gets a laugh.

9. To talk to me, or not to talk to me, that is the question.

    - If the girl has had any descent schooling in her life she'll have to admire your knowledge of Shakespeare and your ability to mack philosophically. For those not well versed in Shakespeare, the actual quote from his play Hamlet is: "To be, or not to be, that is the question."

10. When I was in high school, I used to be the coolest guy in my class.

    - Most likely you probably weren't but if you were, congratulations.
    - You can follow this up after her brief laugh with: "Well, I wasn't the coolest then, but I'm the coolest now" or "So how cool are you?"

11. Why is it that girls are always falling in love with me?

    - A little bit of bravado is ok here because you're speaking of love and not sexual conquests. If she believes you she'll be intrigued why so many girls have had interest in you.

12. If you had a calendar, I'd buy five.

    - Here you are killing two birds with one stone: indirectly paying her a compliment and busting out a little humor.

13. Do you think Michael Jackson is really from the moon and that's why he does that moonwalk dance of his?

   - Waxing philosophically on Michael Jackson is always going to evoke a smile and interesting conversation.

14. Where have you been my whole life?

   - In an indirect way you're telling a girl that she is perfect and what girl is not going to appreciate a compliment like that.

15. I had Lucky Charms this breakfast and I guess they're working.

   - You can follow this up with: "You look magically delicious."

16. Can I ask you a personal question? Which do you think is better: Coca Puffs or Count Chocula?

   - If this girl doesn't know breakfast cereals you are stuck, but if she is in the know she'll find your sugar cereal ponderings quite hilarious.

17. What would you do for a thousand dollars?

   - This is an interesting question that has sexual undertones. If she calls you on its provocative nature, tell her: "Sex is the farthest thing from my mind. I'm just trying to make provocative conversation."

18. Do I have food on over my face because some girl just came over and licked it?

   - It's always good to let a girl know that other women find it necessary to lick you.

19. Did you have major cosmetic surgery or are you just that hot by genetics?

   - If you don't get a laugh at least you know she had major cosmetic surgery.

20. I'm the best.

   - Your gall will command her respect. If she asks "best at what?" you can say: "that's my secret" or "exactly what you're thinking."

   - Some girls are intrigued by the bravado and ultra-confidence of this line.

21. Why do I need to be a good Christian when Heaven is right here before me?

   • Busting out humor, philosophy, and an indirect compliment is a sure way to make a woman melt in your hands and in your mouth.

22. If beauty could kill, you would be a murderer.

   • Win her over with this compliment and dark humor.

23. If beauty was a coffee, you would be a Starbucks.

   • If she's a fan of Starbucks, which most coffee drinkers are, then she is sure to recognize this compliment.

24. If beauty was a car, you would be a Bentley.

   • If she's not familiar with cars, let her in on the fact that a Bentley is a $250,000 hand made British automobile that only the rich of the rich are able to drive.

25. I don't know how I can see because your beauty is blinding.

   • A little cheesy, but much better than "you look hot."

26. If beauty was a mustard, you would be Grey Poupon.

   • If she doesn't crack a smile remind her that Grey Poupon is the mustard of mustards, the fine mustard of the rich.

27. If beauty was a hotel, you would be a Ritz Carlton.

   • If she doesn't smile, remind her that the Ritz Carlton makes the Hilton look like a crack house.

28. If you believe in fairy tales, kiss me and I'll turn into a beautiful prince.

   • She'll laugh at your forwardness and if you're lucky she might even kiss you.

29. I think you drove past me on the freeway last year. Did you?

   • Absolutely a nutty pick-up line, but if she has a sense of humor she'll be laughing.

30. It's either my cologne or your perfume, but something smells amazing.

31. Do I look fat in these jeans?

   - This line gets a laugh because obviously that's what girls ask each other. Spin around and shake your ass for extra laughs.

32. How many gay men have you turned straight?

   - You can't give a woman a better compliment than this. If she doesn't get it, you don't want someone that stupid anyway.

33. Does your oven get jealous of you?

   - If she doesn't get it then respond with: "You know, because you are hotter."

34. Given the same personality, would you rather have your man be thin and poor, or fat and rich?

   - Waxing philosophically should win you some points especially with the humor attached. Could lead into a great conversation about the importance of physical attraction in a relationship.

35. (To a girl wearing a wedding ring): I see that ring on your finger. Have you been cheating on me?

   - Personally I wouldn't mess with a married woman for fear of being OJed but if you fear nothing then this is a funny approach.

36. How does it feel to be the hottest girl in the world?

   - This is a stunning compliment and a great question.

37. If you were a city, you would be Paris.

   - Hopefully she's into making videos too!
   - For those in the don't know: Paris, France is world renowned for its beauty.

38. If beauty was a software company, you would be Microsoft.

   - She'll be amazed at your extraordinary way that you pay a compliment or she might think you're a computer geek. Be careful!

39. You complete me. Do I complete you?

    - Nothing can crack a smile like using the classic quote from the movie "Jerry Maguire."

40. Have you heard of the reality show called "My Life?" Would you like to be in it?

    - You can follow this up with: "You would be my love interest."
    - You can follow this up with: "It's like the other reality shows in that it's real but it's not filmed. It's just my life."

41. Can you hear me now?

    - This is stale Verizon humor, but used upon a girl that is slightly inebriated you are sure to evoke a drunken laugh or burp.

42. I double-dog dare you to kiss me right now!

    - If she's drunk and fairly attracted to you, she might go for it. If she hesitates tell her: "I didn't know they let chickens in this place."

43. Do you think I look more like James Bond or Indiana Jones?

    - If God spent a little more time with you then maybe you do look like one of these handsome fellows however just having the gall to suggest that you do will evoke a laugh.

44. What words come to your mind when you see me: Stud or Sexy-Mother-Fucker?

    - This is a no lose situation as long as the girl isn't a total bitch. By stating two positives you don't even give her a negative to consider.

45. Think about what happens if I'm your destiny, but you blow me off, and the rest off your life turns out for the worse?

    - A dumb girl might be speechless but a girl with relative intelligence is going to at least give it some thought and give you a chance.

46. I might as well ask you right now. Are you going to have a big fit over a prenuptial?

    - This line is funny because you're presuming marriage before you've even met the girl.

47. My mom's ugly. My dad's ugly. So how do you explain this piece of work you have in front of you?

   - Self effacing and yet complimentary to yourself, this pick-up line will no doubt get you a smile and a laugh.

48. They say if your pupils are enlarged that you like or are attracted to the person you're looking at. You must really like me.

   - This line puts the power in your court because it's her pupils that are enlarged (even if they're not) so you're just reacting to her attraction.

49. I've come from the future to save you from the loser you are going to marry. What's my reward: a beer or a kiss?

   - Nothing like a reference from "The Terminator" movies to win the girl over.

50. I bet you can't seduce me.

   - Nothing like putting a girl to a challenge that ends in your own benefit.

51. I can read your mind and you ought to be ashamed of yourself.

   - Once again the ball is in your court. She has to defend herself for thinking such dirty thoughts about you.

52. Do you want to see my tattoo?

   - Even if you don't have one lift up your shirt anyway and say: "Where did it go?"
   - Nothing like setting up the night by showing a little skin with a little silliness. This line is better for men that don't have a huge beer gut, but if you're drunk enough who gives a crap. You'll be respected for your sense of humor nonetheless.

53. I think you should have your own reality show called "The Finest Girl That Ever Lived."

   - Reality shows are more popular than ever and even the dumbest beauty will appreciate this compliment.

54. I'm not a fireman or a cop, but I'll happily dress up as one for you when Halloween comes around.

   • Every woman fantasizes about being with a cop or fireman.

55. I bet you're a terrible kisser. (If she denies it): Then prove it!

   • No girl wants to be a terrible kisser and if she is the wild one in the bunch you had better wake up your tongue.

56. Are you a supermodel?

   • This line will have the best effect on a girl that doesn't fit the typical characteristics of a supermodel.

57. I feel like tipping you and you haven't even done anything but take my breath away.

   • A new spin on a classic pick-up line.

58. My sixth sense tells me that your panties are pink. Is this correct?

   • Slightly aggressive, but if they are pink she'll most likely be very impressed.

59. According to my sixth sense, you are incredibly turned on right now. Am I right?

   • The ball is in your court because now she has to defend herself. Also if she is turned on she will be impressed with your sixth sense.

60. I was reading Nostradamus and he said that you're supposed to fall in love with me tonight. Are you ready to fall in love?

   • For those in the don't know: Nostradamus (1503-66) was a French astrologer/psychic who is known to have predicted Hitler and many other world events that occurred after his death. This line is better suited for a woman that looks like she has a modicum of intelligence.

61. What's that saying about guys with big hands (show hands)?

   • Women will be impressed with your indirect sexual humor and if you have big hands they might be really impressed.

   • For those in the don't know: The saying goes "guys with big hands have big dicks."

62. Is it true that girls just wanna have fun?

    - A funny philosophical question that recalls the classic Cindy Lauper song "Girls Just Wanna Have Fun."

63. Is it true blondes have more fun?

    - Obviously a great question for red heads and brunettes because they are obviously going to want to put in their two cents.

64. Is it true that girls have pillow fights in their panties?

    - A childish question but a question many men have pondered since seeing this phenomenon in many horror movies of the 1980s.

65. (To a girl sitting on a couch): Is that couch comfortable?

    - A great way to downplay your interest in the girl. She will then most likely try to get you more interested in her rather than the couch.

66. (To a girl sitting on a couch): I wish I was that couch you're sitting on.

    - A great indirect-slightly-sexual compliment.

67. You look like the girl that grabbed my butt last weekend. Was that you?

    - Whether you have a nice butt or not is irrelevant. What matters is to put into the girl's mind that some hot girl grabbed your butt last weekend.

68. (To a girl smoking a cigarette): Is that the right size?

    - Obviously a reference to oral sex but when she questions the impropriety of your question you can simply defend yourself by stating that women usually like to smoke longer cigarettes like Marlobro 100s and it looked like a small one.

      NOTE: Studies have said that women who smoke cigarettes are more promiscuous.

69. (To a girl smoking a cigarette): I'm jealous of your cigarette.

    - This could be seen as innocent or sexual depending on the girl but it's a compliment nonetheless.

70. Is it true that women who smoke cigarettes are more promiscuous?

    • Studies have shown that this is true. Women who smoke take part in riskier behavior than those who don't smoke. She will be impressed with your knowledge and it opens an intriguing conversation.

71. (To a girl sitting on a chair): Thanks for saving my spot.

    • Being presumptuous and displaying a touch of bravado always wins over being Mr. Nice Guy.

72. (To a girl sitting on a chair): Oh, we reserved the same chair tonight.

    • Obviously if it's anywhere other than a restaurant you don't reserve chairs and she will appreciate your subtle advance and sense of humor.

73. (To a girl sitting on a chair): Excuse me, but I reserved that chair tonight.

    • Once again one doesn't reserve chairs and unless she had her brain removed she'll crack a smile.

74. (To a girl sitting on a chair): If that chair isn't comfortable, my lap is.

    • Best used on a woman who seems to run a little on the wild side.

75. (To a girl sitting on a chair): That's one lucky chair.

    • Slightly sexual, but on the light side. You will see a smile on her face.

76. (To a girl sitting on a chair): Scoot over.

    • Obviously if there is nowhere to scoot to, she will see your slick wit.

77. (To a girl sitting on a chair): Would you like a lap dance?

    • If she says "yes" you're a lucky man but most likely she will rebuff your offer with a warm smile. If she does say "yes" you better have your lap dance down solid.

78. (To a girl sitting on a chair): $19.99 gets you two lap dances.

    • If she busts out the twenty, get moving.

79. Do you speak Chinese?

    - Wait for her response which ninety-nine percent of the time will be "no" and then reply: "Neither do I, we have a lot in common."

80. It has been said that those who kiss me have great luck afterward. The first one is free.

    - How can she refuse an offer like this?

81. If you're looking for a bad boy, that's me.

    - Younger women are always looking for the "bad boy" so quit posturing and just tell her straight up. You can always just go up to her and lick her face like when Tommy Lee first approached Pamela Anderson.

82. Is it true that women are smarter than men?

    - Even if this is not your personal belief, asking this will put you on her good side immediately. This line can also open a provocative conversation about the battle of the sexes.

83. I'm not happy to see you, I actually have a banana in my pocket.

    - Undeniably funny. If you don't see a smile you might be standing in front of a female suffering from too many nitris hits.
    - Carrying a real banana with you makes this line even more humorous.

84. Do you have the time, because I want to know precisely when I fell in love?

    - Cheesy, but girls from Wisconsin do exist.

85. Do you have lust in your heart?

    - Sometimes you have to get biblical to get a girl's attention.

86. Let's quit playing all the games. Do you want to get married?

    - Given that you just met the girl, a laugh will be heard.

87. You're so hot. Do ever make out with your mirror?

88. (To a girl talking on her cell phone): Is that the president?

   • This line is good for a quick girlie laugh, and when she gets off the phone she'll remember the guy with wit.

89. (To a girl talking on her cell phone): Are you talking to Siegfried and Roy?

90. You take my breadth away. Do you know mouth-to-mouth resuscitation?

   • If the girl is really gullible you might just end up swapping saliva.

91. I saw you playing with your hair over there. Were you flirting with me or were you just playing with your hair?

   • It has been said that when a girl plays with her hair she is subconsciously flirting.

92. Today's my birthday! Will you spank me?

   • Try to use this on a girl who looks like she's into S&M for the maximum success. Also who cares if it's not your birthday, she doesn't need to know that.

93. If I was Superman, your ass would be Kryptomite.

   • Superman is back in style now with that 3 Doors Down song "Krytomite" and the WB television drama "Smallville" so she will definitely be able to relate.

94. Your place or mine.

   • If she says "mine" you had better put on two rubbers because any girl that is good to go that quick probably has more diseases than a Kiss groupie. If the girl has some morality she will laugh at your silly presumptuousness.

95. If it makes any difference I'm one quarter black.

   • Penis size has always been a favorite taboo topic in society, and if size does matter to her then she'll be very impressed.

96. My price is totally negotiable however what do you think about ten dollars?

   • With the recent comedy "Deuce Bigalow Male Gigolo" male prostitution finally got the attention it much deserved. If she whips out a twenty I would take it.

97. The only difference between me and Brad Pitt is that he is better looking, has a cool job, famous, and has more money. So do you want to go out?

   - The important point here is that you put Brad Pitt and yourself in the same sentence which is sure to win you a smile.

98. If you could be a superhero, which one would you be?

   - After she gives her response a great follow up is: "Well Superman and Spiderman are pretty bad ass, but I would rather be Yourman." Doh!

99. I hope you brought your sunglasses because my beauty is bright tonight.

   - Bravado with cheese is a great appetizer for a woman.

100. Rumor has it that you were conceived in a laboratory. An experiment by scientists trying to create the most beautiful woman in the world. Is this true?

   - A stupendous compliment that should get you a beer on her.

101. I have a sixth sense and I sensed that you wanted to know everything about me. Is this true?

   - A tad bit presumptuous but what I've learned in life is it's best to assume the best.

102. Your parents must be hot because you are steaming.

   - Nothing like dishing out compliments to three different people at once.

103. If you were a cigarette you would be a Benson & Hedges.

   - Smoking's popularity has gone up and down over the years but whether she's a smoker or not, remind her that Benson & Hedges is one of the finest cigarettes.

104. Do you speak Latin?

   - When she says "no" you can say: "Neither do I, what are the chances?"
   - Nothing like building rapport with a lady by pointing out the fact that you both don't speak a language that is nearly extinct.

105. Shouldn't you be out dating James Bond or Indiana Jones or something?

  - Nothing like building up a girl's ego with bogus movie characters that kick ass.

106. Could I trouble you for a kiss?

  - If you don't make a big deal out of it then maybe she won't either.

107. Those Queer Guys for the Straight Guy came to my house and I let my rot- weiller out.

  - This line is a little full of testosterone but is sure to emit a laugh.

108. Have you ever seen the reality show "Temptation Island?" I'm Temptation (Insert Your Name). Are you tempted?

  - Any reality-show honey will get a good giggle from this pick-up line.

109. Can I bum a kiss off you?

  - If you can bum a cigarette off of someone, then why not a kiss?

110. Can I bum your phone number off you?

111. Can I bum a date off you?

112. Can I bum a fuck off you?

  - The audacity! Watch out for the drink and the slap. Maybe, just maybe, she has an extra one for you.

113. Do you want to do that "Bonnie and Clyde" thing: fall in love and go rob banks?

  - The younger babes may not get this classic movie reference, but if she does know it, she should appreciate a man who's into passion and action.

114. Usted es una mujer muy hermosa y yo soy hermoso también. In Spanish, that means: "You are a very beautiful woman and I am beautiful also."

  - Nothing like showing a woman that you're a gentleman and a worldly man.

115. Vous êtes une très belle femme et je suis beau aussi. In French, that means: "You are a very beautiful woman and I am beautiful also."

- They say French is the language of love. Let's see if it is for you.

116. Lei sono una molto bella donna e sono bell'anche. In Italian, that means: "You are a very beautiful woman and I am beautiful also."

- You may not drive a Ferrari or have Armani suits but that doesn't mean you can't wax an Italian compliment to yourself and a fair lady.

117. Sie sind eine sehr schöne Frau und ich bin schön auch. In German, that means: "You are a very beautiful woman and I am beautiful also."

- Not the prettiest of languages, but the BMW sure has some nice lines.

118. Mi nombre es cualquier usted quiere ser. In Spanish that means: "My name is whatever you want it to be."

- Whether the girl is Spanish or not, she is sure to appreciate a man that can speak a little Spanish and put a spin on an old but classic pick-up line.

119. Mon nom est quoi que vous voulez ez être. In French, that means: "My name is whatever you want it to be."

- If she is digging you later it might be time to introduce her to the word "man-age-a-toi"—the French word for three-some—and grab her friend too.

120. Mi chiamo il cosa di qualunque lei lo vuole essere. In Italian, that means: "My name is whatever you want it to be."

- If she is digging your small Italian vocabulary you can tell her that you don't have a Ferrari but you know how to order pizza.

121. Mein Name ist, was auch immer Sie es wollen, zu sein. In German, that means: "My name is whatever you want it to be."

- If she is digging your German, tell her that you don't drive a Mercedes but you do splurge on Heineken once in a while. However, if you're rich and driving a phat Benz then it wouldn't hurt to drop that information.

   Note: If you are planning on traveling to a foreign country and would like to translate other pick-up lines from *Pick-Up Lines That Work* check out www.freetranslation.com to translate.

122. I think you are my new religion. Do you have a book that I should follow?

   • You can follow this up with: "I bet you have a large congregation don't you?"

123. Can I search your purse (pause), because I think you stole my heart?

   • You'll win her smile when she hears such deft wit.

124. I don't see any bags around here but do you have any baggage?

   • A lot of woman have emotional baggage from past relationships so maybe she'll come clean and tell all now. If you're lucky she'll be baggage free, share a laugh with you, and you'll both live happily ever after.

125. If you were an adjective, you would be gorgeous.

   • You are set to win smiles even if she isn't an English major.

126. I don't have much for breakfast, but my bed is really comfortable.

   • Nothing like sheer confidence to win a girl over.

127. Looks like someone won the beauty lottery.

   • You can follow this up with: "Who had the ticket, you mother or your father?"

128. Do you think we could ever just be friends?

   • This poses the great conundrum question that was addressed in the movie "When Harry Met Sally": Can a man and woman just be friends without sexual tension always budding in? This line can lead into a great conversation.

129. Can I join your fan club?

   • Flattery will get you everywhere with a woman.

130. If I was rich I would fly you around the world and buy you the finest things but I'm dirt poor.

   • Hopefully the girl appreciates comedy and honesty more than money.

131. I have an indecent proposal: a game of tonsil hockey for a dollar.

   - Watch for the slap, but if she has seen the movie "Indecent Proposal" then she will surely crack a smile.

132. I have an indecent proposal: a game of doctor for a dollar.

   - If she balks remind her that the game is a lot cheaper than the real doctor.

133. I have an indecent proposal: a grab of your ass for one dollar.

   - Better make sure she doesn't have a boyfriend around the place that will pummel your ass before you unleash this gutsy pick-up line.

134. I have an indecent proposal: to nibble on your ear for one dollar.

   - She might need a dollar for the ninety-nine-cent store and an ear nibble is pretty innocent.

135. I have an indecent proposal: one night with me and I'll give you twenty dollars.

   - This is best used on the drunken-slutty girl.

136. You're like a little sail boat lost at sea and I'm the big tug boat that's going to pull you into harbor.

   - Nothing like using an analogy to help a girl to see your chivalric ways.

137. I know you've been searching for the perfect guy. Well I'm here!

   - Confidence, confidence, and confidence always wins.

138. Quit looking for Mr. Right, and go with Mr. Right Now.

   - By suggesting this slight shift in thinking, you will win her.

139. Excuse my beauty, my name is (your name).

   - Use this pick-up line for comedic irony especially if you are short on looks.

140. Let's face it, you need me.

   - Sometimes a girl needs to be told what's best for her.

141. Let me be frank. I'm selfish, rude, smoke, psycho, and I'm depressed. Is there still a chance for you and me?

   - If all of these things apply to you then this is not the best pick-up line for you my friend. However if you aren't a head case then this can be a very funny pick-up line. Just be sure to follow it up with: "Just kidding."

142. Can I ask you a personal question? What do you think of my butt?

   - When polled, girls usually rate the butt and stomach as their two favorite body parts on a guy. Even if you don't have a nice ass, it's still a great ice-breaker. Don't be afraid to shake it for an extra laugh.

143. Can I ask you a personal question? Do you think I'm fat?

   - Once again, this is a question that the girls ask each other and when you pose it to her she'll find you hilarious.

144. What kind of animal do you think I look like?

   - If you look carefully, every person resembles an animal whether it be a lizard or a leopard. This can spark a funny conversation and it's less of a direct pick-up line if you want to take a less aggressive stance.

145. Yeah I know I'm not perfect, but I'm working on it.

   - A woman can appreciate a man that can acknowledge his flaws and be humorous at the same time.

146. You know when I die, I probably won't be remembered for any great thing or accomplishment, but I'm OK with that.

   - She will love you for your humor and honesty.

147. If beauty had a copyright, you would be sued for a lot of money.

   - The girl will admire your observation of our litigious society combined with the observation of her beauty.

148. Would you hold it against me if I told you that you were the second prettiest, next to Mother Nature?

   - If the girl asks "Who?" then you should probably move on to the next hot girl.

149. I left my good pick-up lines at home tonight. So what's up?

- Girls love honesty.

150. I'm not dark and handsome, I'm white and heinous.

- Watch for the beer spray from her mouth because if this pick-up line is remotely accurate for you she will not be able to control her laugh reflexes.

151. Who was that geek you were talking to earlier?

- Sure you sound like some bully from high school but maybe she liked the bullies in high school.

152. Have you seen your smile around here?

- If she doesn't smile with this pick-up line she might be suffering from a case of permafrown.

153. I'm not worthy, but can you tell me what time it is?

- You may not be worthy but after you deliver this clever line, you will be.

154. I'm thinking about developing my own cologne called Stud Boy. What do you think?

- Every girl loves an entrepreneur, especially one with a sense of humor.

155. Do you think you have a chance with me?

- This puts the ball in your court. You're the bad ass. Does she have what it takes? Assume mighty confidence and she will believe.

156. Did you come here from another dimension, the Hot Zone?

- If she has never heard of the Twilight Zone don't worry, she'll probably still realize that she is being dished a compliment.

157. What would you do for five dollars?

- If she mentions anything good then I hope you have your money ready. This line can lead to some riveting conversation about the power of money.

158. Are you in the armed forces, because you blow all the other girls away?

- With the world being rife with conflict, she will for sure be impressed with your analogy.

159. If you're looking for a rebound guy, I'm ok with that.

- Whether or not she is looking for a rebound guy, she'll find your pick-up line utterly hilarious.

160. How come girls get to have all the things to make them look prettier and us guys have nothing?

- She will admire your great ponderous mind.

161. Hey, if you're looking for a man that's rich and powerful, that's not me.

- Your brutal honesty will at a minimum win her smile if not her heart.

162. If you're looking for a tough guy, I can act tough.

- Subconsciously all girls are looking for a guy that can protect them from danger. The fact that you're stating your abilities up front is bound to score you some points.

163. What would you say is your level of attraction to me: powerful, strong, undeniable, or unbreakable?

- Once again when you present her with all positives it makes it much harder for her to see you in a negative light and you'll also come across with a sense of humor.

164. I wouldn't meet your normal qualifications for a date but what are your qualifications for late-night bootie call?

- Remember, you can always work your way up from bootie call.

165. You look like a man-eater, but I'm not scared.

- Paying a woman a compliment but also showing your courage is a great way to go.

166. Do you see me more as date material or bootie call?

  • One is better than the other but either way you are still getting some action.

167. Your prayers have been answered.

  • If she seems confused you can follow it up with: "Haven't you been praying for Mr. Right Now?"

168. The first time is free.

  • She can interpret this anyway she would like too, that's what's great about it.

169. I don't mind being used as long as you're up front about it.

  • A refreshing thing for a woman to hear since it's women that are usually complaining about being used.

170. Have you seen a smile around here?

  • Somewhat stupid, but you're almost guaranteed a smile from the girl.

171. I don't kiss and tell.

  • This line is so forward that it's funny.

172. If you were a watch, you would be a Rolex.

  • The girl will love you for your compliment and knowledge of fine watches.

173. Am I on drugs, or are you that fine?

  • This works better if you don't look like you are on drugs or wasted off of Amstel Light.

174. If you have a boyfriend, I think he'll understand.

  • Sometimes you need to help a girl justify doing a bad thing.

175. I don't want to be your boyfriend, I want to be your MANFRIEND!

  • Maybe she's dating a boy and needs to step up to your plate, or maybe she will just admire your play on words.

176. I don't want to be your boyfriend, I want to be your MANLOVER.

  • Sometimes honesty works best with a woman.

177. If I can guess one digit in your phone number will you give it to me?

  • If she says "no," then bust out a joke. However if she says "yes," it's time to tap your sixth sense.

178. If I can guess two digits in your phone number will you give it to me?

  • If she says "yes," I would go for the digits in the local area code.

179. If I can guess three digits in your phone number will you give it to me?

  • Once again if she says "yes," go for the local area code.

180. Would it be too much to ask for you make me dinner tomorrow night?

  • Bold and brash, but you will win points for your audacity.

181. Aren't you hot in those clothes?

  • This line is best delivered for maximum comical delivery if used when a girl isn't wearing much to begin with.

182. You're going to make me make the first move huh?

  • The ball is in your court because you're making the assumption that she likes you. Always a good move.

183. What kind of car do you drive?

  • You are sure to win a smile when you throw the role reversal on her. Put the pressure on her to impress you!

184. Player is such a dirty word. I prefer to be called indecisive.

  • You are sure to win her affection with your unique point of view.

185. After twelve midnight my price goes back up to ten bucks.

  • Playing with the concept of male prostitution is sure to elicit innocent laughs.

186. Where's your line at?

- Once again you retain the power by calling her out and putting the pressure on her. This can backfire, but the advantages to you are twofold. First, it takes pressure off you. Second, you come across as confident.

- If she says "What line?" you can respond with: "Your line to hit on me with."

187. I'm an amateur masseuse. Would you like a rub?

- Everybody likes a massage and some comedy to go with it.

188. The nation should honor you with a national holiday. They should call it National Hot Girl Day.

- We are all waiting for this holiday to come.

189. Are we going to keep playing games or are you going to ask me out?

- Put the power in your court and presume she likes you.

190. I don't care if those are contact lenses, your eyes are intoxicating.

- A lot of the girls these days are wearing fake colored lenses. Whether her's are real or not, you're still paying her a compliment along with a touch of humor.

191. I know the boys have let you down, but a man has arrived to save you.

- This is a perfect way to set yourself apart from your competition, just make sure you back up your bold words. Puff out your chest for an extra smile.

192. When I say no, I mean no.

- Coming from a woman's mouth this is serious business, but when you say it as an opening line, there is no way to interpret it but hilarious.

193. When I say no, I really mean yes.

- Once again, this is typically a woman's phrase but when delivered from a man's mouth it will bring smiles to all femme fatales.

194. Did you come from the future to save me from some heartless bitch?

- This is another spin on "The Terminator" movie with a little more bite.

195. Do you bite?

- No woman wants to appear mean so she will attempt to convince you otherwise.

196. I want someone to want me for my mind and not just for my body.

- Once again, these words that usually come from a woman's mouth will be heard as quite humorous coming from yours.
- This line is most effective if you are out of shape.

197. What do you think of polygamy?

- Polygamy, known as marriage to multiple women, will evoke passionate responses from some women. Regardless, it makes for interesting conversation.

198. Tall, dark, and handsome I am not, but I am here to save your day.

- If you are indeed not tall, dark, and handsome then there is a good chance from your previously stated truths that the girl will believe that you will truly save her day.

199. I have no problem at all to be on your backup-bootie-call list.

- This humorous pick-up line might graduate you to her primary bootie-call list.

200. Quit playing games and just tell me that you love me.

- This absurdity and presumption will win you a smile.

201. Do you like your eggs scrambled or over easy?

- Your presumptuous assumption that the girl will spend the night and have breakfast will get you a laugh. However it might go over her head and she might think you're just asking a simple question about how she likes her eggs.

202. I bet even when you look bad you still look good.

   • Great pick-up line, but you may be surprised when her makeup comes off.

203. What's your benefits package?

   • Nothing like having a woman compare herself to a company.

204. Do you know I won the world's best kisser contest?

   • Obviously she knows you're probably lying but when she doubts you, you can say something like: "Pucker your lips and I'll prove it to you."

205. What's so lucky about Lucky Charms? I eat them and nothing ever happens.

   • This line just goes for the quick laugh and a little sympathy.

206. Do you think it's slutty to make out with a stranger?

   • If she says "no" then say: "Let's make out." If she says "yes" then say: "Me too. Who would of known that we would have so much in common."

   • This line is best used in a party atmosphere where alcohol is involved. Studies have shown that if a woman is already in a horny mood that alcohol will make her even hornier.

207. Do you think my clothes make a statement that I'm rich and successful (pause), because I'm not.

   • This just goes for the quick laugh.

208. I was going to be a doctor or a lawyer and then I said to myself: Does money really create happiness?

   • This line opens the floor for an interesting conversation about money and happiness.

209. If you're one of those people that believe things happen for a reason, how do you explain me?

Chapter 3
Bar Pick-Up Lines

The bar is the most popular place to pick up women and it's definitely one of the best. Women come to the bar to party and to meet men. What more could you ask for in an environment? There are more single woman at bars and nightclubs than any other environment. Another reason that the bar is a perfect environment for picking up women is the alcohol.

Alcohol used in moderation works to your advantage. First, it loosens your inhibitions and will make it slightly easier to approach women. The drinks as they say "take the edge off." Second, alcohol is known to intensify one's emotions. For example if a girl is feeling horny, she will feel hornier. If a girl is feeling happy, she will feel happier. If a girl is depressed, she will feel more depressed. Watch out for those!

The bar is the best place to perfect your pick-up techniques while having a great time with your friends at the same time. The only negative factor about the bars is the number of guys that you're competing against, but if you have the flawless PJCSP pick-up formula down solid you'll leave your competition in the dust. Go get them!

1. Do you like Blow Jobs or Sex on the Beach, and I'm talking about the drinks of course?

    • If she says "Who cares about the drinks" you are on your way to a good night.

2. I had this dream last night and I was here in this bar and you were here too. What do think that means?

    • She may think you're full of crap, but if she half believes you she'll be intrigued. This pick-up line can also lead to a provocative conversation about dream interpretation.

3. I'm letting girls do body shots off my chiseled torso for five dollars. How many can I count you in for?

    -   If you do have a chiseled torso then you'll probably make a lot of money. If you don't have a chiseled torso then you'll probably make a lot of laughs. Either way you're a winner.

4. I'll buy you a beer if you promise to hang out with me all night and tell the other girls how hot and cool I am.

    -   If she takes your proposition seriously then it's great to have girl around to spread the word of your greatness. If she just laughs that's not bad either. Either way you win.

5. James Bond came up to me and asked me how I do it and I said: "James, it takes more than a shaken martini and a tuxedo my friend."

    -   Putting yourself on a tier higher than James Bond takes balls, but every girl will respect your audacity.

6. Why is it that we have to pollute our body with chemicals like alcohol and tobacco to have a good time?

    -   A stimulating question that could lead to an interesting conversation on escaping reality.

7. You know I did you a favor and interviewed all the guys in this joint and they're all losers.

    -   If she believes you, great. If not she will appreciate your sense of humor.

8. Did you bring your beer goggles tonight because two hours from now I might be your prince charming?

    -   For those in the don't know: Beer goggles are the warped vision of grandeur one gets of the opposite sex when one is inebriated.

9. There is used to be this gay bartender here who used to give me free beer. Do you think he liked me or liked me liked me?

    -   This shows that a gay man was attracted to you and subconsciously the girl will think you are more attractive.

10. Do you think there is beer in heaven?

   • This is a question which she will contemplate with a smile. This line can lead to a provocative conversation about the afterlife.

11. Here we are, two strangers in a bar, probably nothing in common, what do you think the chances are that it's our destiny to fall in love?

   • She'll respect your honesty and your ability to flirt with the idea of destiny. Could lead to a fruitful conversation about fate.

12. Why is it that Hollywood needs cocaine to have fun? I think this Bud Light is just fine.

   • If she asks "What's wrong with cocaine?" you might want to move on to the next girl unless you want a future junkie coming over and stealing your DVD player.

13. Can you break a hundred?

   • When she says "no," a good playful response is: "I just wanted to see if you were rich." Once again this is a play on role reversal. It's a mindfuck for girls because they're usually thinking that guys want them just for their bodies.

14. Can you break a thousand?

   • When she says "no," a good playful response is: "I just wanted to see if you were rich."

15. In antiquity my beer gut would have been a sign of prosperity and attractiveness. What do you think it represents today?

   • In antiquity most people were thin due to the scarcity of food. The fat were seen as the most desirable mates because it was indicative of their wealth.

16. My buddy said you were checking me out. How bad do you want me?

   • This is a nice way to deflect your interest.

17. I can't believe they don't serve Everclear here.

   • If you are trying to look like a bad ass this is a great statement because Everclear is known to be one-hundred percent alcohol.

18. Did you steal my beer because that looks just like the one I was drinking?

   • If she gets defensive just respond: "Listen I won't call the cops if you just give me your phone number."

19. You know Benjamin Franklin said: "Beer is proof that God loves us and wants us to be happy." Do you think God drinks beer?

   • This is a true statement by Benjamin Franklin which can strike up profound conversation about higher powers along with a few good laughs.

20. When you were growing up did you ever dream that the man of your dreams was a drunk?

   • She will say "no" and at that point you can reply: "Well I'm not a drunk, but I am drunk with your beauty."

21. Are you here for a supermodel convention?

   • Every girl at some point wished that they had the beauty of a model, so with this compliment you will win her affection as long as you deliver it sincerely.

22. If I guess your weight will you buy me a beer?

   • Weight can be a sensitive topic with women and that's why you will want to use this line on a woman who is thin. Used upon a thin chick she will likely play along and you might even get a free beer out of it.

23. If I guess your weight and your age will you sleep with me tonight?

   • Although you might sound like a circus worker, you will definitely get yourself a laugh and/or a smile.

24. If you guess my weight I'll buy you a beer.

   • This is a no lose situation for a girl, but you better have the money to pay up if she guesses it correctly.

25. If you guess my age I'll buy you a beer.

   • Another fun spin on the guessing game.

26. If you guess my age and weight I'll buy you a beer.

27. I live underneath the freeway. How about yourself?

   • If she doesn't get this joke she'll probably run from you, but as long as the girl has a sense of humor she will bust out a smile for you.

28. I don't mean to brag, but I got paid today and I have a crisp twenty in my wallet.

   • Hopefully she can appreciate sarcasm or this line isn't going to work for you.

29. Somebody grabbed my butt a minute ago. Was that you?

   • Personally I love the butt-grab question because not only do you have the power but it also says that girls want to grab your butt. How can you lose? Just make sure you say it with a smile.

   Note: Anytime when you use a pick-up line that puts a girl on the defensive such as "Did you just grab my butt?" or "My buddy said you were checking me out" it's ultra-important to display a smile and use body language that says you're into her. If she doesn't sense your warmth you'll get rejected out of defense of her own ego.

30. I got this email that said to be here at this bar and talk to the girl in the red dress (or whatever the hot girl is wearing).

   • She'll either be intrigued or think you're full of crap but she'll appreciate your originality regardless.

31. I keep trying to drink my beer but you're too distracting.

   • What girl doesn't like to be distracting? Get ready for a warm smile with this line.

32. You know I came in this bar an hour ago and saw you, and here you are again. Are you stalking me?

   • Since stalking is a male dominated crime chances are she'll see the humor in your pick-up line.

33. My buddy said you were looking at my ass. Do you want to touch it?

   • If she gets defensive a great response is: "Listen, I'm flattered," or "It's nothing to be ashamed about."

34. My psychic told me to talk to the hottest chick in the bar. Do you have a message for me?

   • The girl will be flattered with the compliment and everyone these days seems to be intrigued by psychics.

35. If your beauty was alcoholic I'd be getting my stomach pumped right about now.

   • Hopefully the girl will see this metaphorical compliment in the positive light that it's meant to be seen in.

36. I'm having a make out contest tonight and whomever French kisses the best gets a free beer. Are you in?

   • You'll either get a laugh out of your outrageousness or a nice kiss. Either way you come out a winner.

37. I have an idea for a reality series: "Me and The Hot Chick From the Bar." What do you think?

   • She'll love you for you compliment and your creative mind.

38. (Pull up your shirt): What you see is what you get.

   • If you are ripped she'll no doubt be impressed. If you are built like the Pillsbury DoughBoy it's at least good for a girlie giggle.

39. (To two girls talking): Hey, quit fighting over me, I like both of you.

   • Your assuredness will grant you smiles.

40. (To two girls talking): Quit fighting over me, it's embarrassing.

   • Hot girls are always dumbfounded if you aren't immediately captivated with them so if you tell them that they're embarrassing they'll be captivated by you.

41. (To two girls talking and with you grabbing your butt): No these aren't butt implants.

   • Women will love you for your confidence and your bravado.

42. Were you looking at that girl's butt?

   • A provocative question regardless of her answer. This line can lead to a great conversation about lesbianism.

43. Want to feel my boobs?

   • This would be a taboo question for a female to ask a man but not the other way around. Go for it and see the smiles and smirks.

44. Is the Internet the only thing that you surf?

   Hopefully she's a mansurfer too, but that will be for her to disclose to you. Most likely she won't understand the sexual connotations behind the question.

45. I have a huge bed but I like it on the floor. How about yourself?

   • A girl can take this question as she likes. She can view it as innocent as in your sleeping preferences or if her mind is more on the dirty side she will see it as your sexual preferences. Either way it initiates bedroom conversation.

46. Who's this Snoop Doggy-Style guy?

   • With this pick-up line you have to play the moron so you don't seem like you're making a cheap sex reference. If you play the dumb guy well, you will get a laugh from the girl.

47. What time do the body shots start?

   • This is better used for a girl that is wearing something revealing or attention getting.

48. Could you do me a favor and flirt with the bar tender and get me a few free drinks?

   • This is great if you want to strike up a conversation without coming on strong but still displaying a sense of humor.

49. If I guess your name in three guesses, you buy me a beer. If not I'll buy you a beer. Are you in?

   • A fun game to get the conversation started.

50. If I guess your name in three guesses, will you buy me a beer?

    • If you want to win her affection, go for beautiful names with significance such as Cinderella (beautiful fairy tale girl), Giselle (Leonardo DiCaprio's supermodel girlfriend), and Belle(French word for beautiful).

51. Most women are intimidated by me. Are you so intimidated that you won't buy me a beer?

    • Nothing like bullying a woman into buying you a beer.

52. I'm thinking about opening a bar called Midget Circus where a bunch of midgets are juggling and riding unicycles on the bar. What do you think?

    • She'll either find this line extremely hilarious or extremely offensive. You'll have to try to pinpoint the likelihood of her response before you ask.

53. I'm thinking about opening a bar called Crazy Orgy where everybody gets drunk and has sex. What do you think?

    • This pick-up line is best used on a woman who looks like she would frequent a bar called Crazy Orgy.

54. I couldn't help but notice that you were drinking the same beer as me. Are you trying to copy me?

    • Nothing like trying to win a girl over by pointing out your similarities.

55. So how long have you been drinking Bud Light (or whatever beer she's drinking)?

    • She is sure to crack a smile when talking about her alcoholic beverage consumption history.

56. In my religion hedonism, it's OK for us to have a one-night stand.

    • Anything you can due to make a woman feel better about a one-night stand is to your advantage.

    • For those in the don't know: Hedonism is the devotion to pleasure and self-gratification as a way of life.

57. Are you famous, because I see all these people coming up and talking to you?

   • Everybody likes to feel important and she'll love the fact that you think she's famous.

58. How many have you had? Beers that is?

   • Just when she's thinking you're talking about her sex life, you throw a curveball at her and make it innocent. She'll love you for your play of words.

59. Let's play "Fear Factor!" You take off your clothes and run around the bar and I'll give you a dollar.

   • When she balks raise the ante to five dollars.

60. Let's play "Massage Factor!" You give me a massage while I drink my beer.

   • If she hasn't seen the television show "Fear Factor" hopefully she'll still find humor in the line anyway.

61. Let's play "Fear Factor!" You blow fireballs with 151 and I'll give you a dollar.

   • If she's psycho enough to do it, don't catch your hair on fire.

62. Let's play "Fear Factor!" You go make out with the ugliest guy in the bar and I'll give you a dollar.

   • If she takes you up on your Fear Factor Challenge, then who knows what she'll do for five dollars.

63. Truth or Dare: Truth—Is it true you've been admiring my every move tonight?

   • For those in the don't know: Truth or Dare is a classic game in which the participants put each other up to a truth or dare.

   • If she balks at the "truth" then say: "I dare you to give me your phone number."

64. Truth or Dare: Dare—I dare you to buy me a beer.

   • Free beer is good beer.

65. Truth or Dare: Dare—I dare you to mount this bar and strip like you're at Girls Girls Girls.

    • Hopefully you're talking to a girl that doesn't like to lose.

66. Truth or Dare: Truth—Have you ever felt an attraction this strong?

    • If she says "yes," then respond with: "Lying is not permitted in this game."

67. When you get done with that beer are we going to play spin the bottle?

    • Nothing wrong with evoking innocent childhood games when you're an adult.

68. Is it hot in here or is it just you?

    • This is better suited for the young girls because the older ones might have heard this line a few hundred times.

69. Is it hot in here or is it just me?

    • This is a great spin on the tried and true classic. This type of self-approving line is better received by one that wasn't blessed with model-like features.

70. I have an indecent proposal: buy me a beer.

    • If women ever want to be truly equal in society they need to start buying more beers.

71. Is there something wrong with the smoke alarms here?

    • If she says "Why?" you can follow up with: "Because you are a four-alarm fire."

72. Excuse me ma'am I'm going to have to write you a ticket because the sign on the door says "No 10s aloud."

    • Most women would never be considered a perfect 10 so most women will be appreciate such a compliment. However, beware of the feminists out there who are offended by such chauvinistic scales.

73. (To a girl holding or drinking a Coors Light): Would you hold it against me if I told you I prefer Bud Light over Coors Light?

   • This could lead to a provocative conversation about light beers.

74. Before you got here the bar did an independent unbiased survey and I'm the best guy here.

   • If she believes you, you are set. If not at least you'll get yourself a smile from your silliness.

75. You should come out with your own perfume called Hot Bar Girl.

   • If she runs with your idea make sure you get a cut of the proceeds.

76. If I owned a bar you would be on the VIP list.

77. (To a girl holding a drink): Are you going to finish that?

   • She'll love your audacity. If she happens to say "no," then grab it and finish it off. If she says "yes," you can say: "I love a girl that finishes what she starts."

78. If there was dancing here I would ask you to dance.

   • She will be flattered with your thoughtful contemplation.

79. I've been waiting for my turn all night.

   • Nothing like displaying to a girl your aptitude for patience.

80. (Hold up your beer): Want to race?

   • Beer racing is commonly known in the fraternities but not to the common woman. She will be intrigued with your humor and odd challenge.

81. At 2:00 a.m. if you still haven't found anyone good, I'll be over here.

   • Sometimes with the right girl it will work to your advantage to play the nonchalant role. Some girls are intrigued by guys that play it cool.

82. You want a drink? (Wait until she says "yes.") Me too. Can you get me a Long Island Ice Tea and a beer?

   • She'll laugh at your outrageousness.

83. You know I just want to warn you that I don't look nearly this good in the morning.

    • A woman's phrase emitted from a man's mouth will result in a laugh.

84. I haven't had a beer all night but I'm drunk with your beauty.

    • She'll love your ability to mix a compliment with your surroundings.

85. Your beauty is intoxicating.

    • Once again she'll love your choice of adjective considering your location.

86. Are you cold like your beer?

    • This is best used on a girl that seems upbeat because a girl that looks like she's in a bad mood will likely take offence and not see the humor behind it.

87. If you were a drink what would be the name of it?

    • This is fun for a girl because it allows her to be creative. Open-ended questions that demand her involvement are always good.

88. I don't think the men tonight need to worry about getting beer drunk but with you around they need to worry about getting love drunk.

89. And I thought the beer was good here.

90. Are you a professional beer drinker?

91. If you drank a beer for every guy that checked you out, you would be passed out right now.

92. I bet if church had beer and gambling a lot more people would show up. What do you think?

    • This is best used on a girl that looks more promiscuous than religious.

93. Can I ask you a personal question? Bud or Bud Light?

94. For the price of that beer you could have had me for the night.

Chapter 4
Car Pick-Up Lines

Picking up a woman in your car is difficult but not impossible. You have to make the most out of the time given to you. You must move from pick-up line to phone number very quickly. Once you have unleashed one of the eighty-three Car Pick-Up Lines below you can quickly follow up with one of the these closers:

- "I don't want to lose you forever, what's your phone number?"

- "I want a second date, what's your phone number?"

- "If I'm your destiny, I'm going to need your phone number."

Since time is not in your favor you had better have your pen and paper or cell phone at your fingertips. Go get them!

1. People really pay attention to these traffic lights huh?

    - You will evoke a smile when you poke fun at something as serious as the observance of traffic lights.

2. (Pointing at the traffic light): Don't you think red, white, and blue would be a little more patriotic than green, yellow, and red?

    - Sometimes stupid is funny.

3. You want to race?

    - Girls aren't used to a challenge of this nature which will win you a laugh.

4. My Ferrari is at home, it draws too much attention to me.

    - A little white lie doesn't hurt anyone when comedy is involved.

5. (To a girl driving a Volkswagon): Do you have any idea what that Volk-swagon Farfugnugen thing was about?

    - For those in the don't know: "Farfugnugen" was a silly word that Volk-swagon used in their old advertising campaigns. No one ever really knew what this weird "Farfugnugen" thing was really about. She will smile at your sense of humor.

    - This is best used on a girl (twenty-five or older) who was around when this advertising campaign was running.

6. I like your driving. What do you think of mine?

    - This is not a comment a woman usually hears so it'll be music to her ears.

7. Your such a courteous driver. Do you teach Driver's Education?

8. Do I have food on my face because women keep staring at me when they drive by?

    - This is a tricky way of telling a woman that you are a man in demand albeit in a silly way.

9. I drink and drive, but just with coffee.

    - She'll appreciate your comic relief on such a serious topic.

10. What do you think my car says about me?

    - Cars definitely make a statement about the person behind the wheel and this pick-up line will get her thinking about you.

11. Excuse me, can you tell me the quickest way to get to your bedroom?

12. I gave my Mercedes away to a homeless person. Do you want to go out?

    - She probably won't believe you but if the saying "it's the thought that counts" holds true, you should win some points with her.

13. Have you seen Knight Rider around here? That guy owes me money.

    - Young girls won't get this reference to one of the best television crime fighting shows of the 1980s involving David Hasselhoff and his talking car Kit.

14. Come here often?

   • Obviously the comedy lies here in the fact that you are moving or at a temporary stop, not a destination.

15. Have you ever maxed that baby out?

   • Girls don't max their cars out unless they're on a high-speed chase from the cops so you'll definitely receive a smile from this pick-up line.

16. Were you really fixing your hair or were you flirting with me?

   • Girls do flirt with their hair and if you catch her in the act then assume the positive and assume that you're her prince charming.

17. You need a push?

   • Of course her car is working fine but she'll enjoy your joshing humor.

18. I bet I can get to my place faster than you.

   • So stupid and obvious that you'll have her in stitches.

19. Are you sure you're old enough to drive that thing?

   • This is better used on a woman who is older and would appreciate looking sixteen again.

20. Ma'am this is a city street, not the Indy 500.

   • This is ideal for a woman that is accelerating or breaking fast. She will appreciate your acute observation.

21. 2 Fast 2 Furious!

   • If she is in her late teens or early twenties she'll probably understand this comedic reference to the Hollywood racecar movie "2 Fast 2 Furious."

22. How am I suppose to flirt with you when you're driving so crazy?

   • This is used for best comedic affect if she's not driving crazy at all.

23. Is it my car you're after or ME?

   • This works hilariously well if the car you're driving is a piece of crap.

24. It's kind of hard to kiss when all of this metal and distance is between us.

   • She'll crack a smile at your ludicrous presumptuousness.

25. I just drive this piece of shit because I don't want to get carjacked.

   • She'll love your humorous justification of your poverty-stricken ride.

26. Are you listening to self-help tapes in there?

   • You'll get your smile with this comment due to the fact that most hot young women aren't going to be driving around listening to self-help tapes.

27. You want to play bumper cars?

   • If you happen to be talking to a crazy person you had better watch out.

28. Are you headed to the beauty pageant?

   • Women love to be beautiful and the suggestion will win you a smile.

29. Shouldn't you have a driver?

   • If the girl has a descent self esteem she'll assume that you mean she should be in the back of a limo.

30. Is the limo in the shop?

   • The woman will appreciate that you think she is so hot that she should be driven by a limo.

31. Is that yours or did you carjack that ride?

   • The fact that women very rarely carjack people will surely win you a laugh and a smile.

32. I was about to have some road rage and then I saw you.

   • The girl will feel special that her beauty prevented your violent vehicle temper tantrum.

33. I don't work on cars but I work on women. Do you need a tune-up?

   • This will work best on women that look a little on the wild side.

34. BMW may be the ultimate driving machine but I'm the ultimate woman dream.

    • Best used on a girl driving a BMW who will appreciate your knowledge of the BMW slogan "the ultimate driving machine" in addition to your comedic twist.

35. Are you headed to my house?

36. Your car is a lucky machine.

37. Your window is down, my window is down, some may view it as coincidence, but I think it's destiny.

    • Your ridiculous view on destiny will put her in stitches.

38. Have you driven a hunk lately?

    • For those in the don't know: This is a spin off the Ford slogan: "Have you driven a Ford lately?"

39. Do you need a boyfriend change?

    • If she doesn't catch the reference to oil change then you might be better off trying this line on the next hot girl.

40. If you're going to crash, crash at my place.

    • She'll love your understanding of the multiple meanings of the word "crash."

41. Have you ever heard that Dave Matthew's song "Crash Into Me?" Well don't get any ideas.

    • She'll love your spin on pop music.

42. What time are you do back at the mental hospital?

    • Dark comedy will often win you the biggest laugh when picking up a woman.

43. Are you following me (pause), because I don't mind?

44. Normally I don't like people to tailgate me, but you can tailgate me all night long.

45. Where's your helmet?

   • Most people haven't worn a helmet since their mom made them wear one when they were little riding their tricycles. If she picks one off her seat to show you, then be very afraid.

46. So how many cars have you wrecked?

   • So many pretty girls are used to getting compliments on their looks that sometimes you can win them over by slighting them. Just make sure you are wearing your winning smile.

47. Can you do a wheelee in that thing?

   • If she busts a wheelee for you who knows what can of crazy tricks she can do in bed.

48. If gas mileage was based on beauty you would never have to fill up again.

49. I know this excellent place we can park and pretend it's the 1960s. What do you say?

   • For those in the don't know: In the 1960s "parking" was synonymous with "parking the car and making out."

50. I bet your car insurance is high just because your hotness is likely to distract others and cause more accidents. Am I right?

51. Do you need a tune-up?

52. You must be lost, because my place is the opposite direction.

53. How are your bags, air bags that is?

   • This works for maximum comedic value if the girl has some big tits.

54. You're making me overheat.

   • If she seems to be down with you, follow up with: "Do you think you can pull over and check me out?"

55. The pedal on the right is the gas.

    • Sometimes pointing out the obvious to a woman will win you an easy smile.

56. Have you ever ridden in a Ford (or any inexpensive car you might be driving) before?

    • She'll love your sarcasm and self-effacing humor.

57. (To a girl at a red light): Excuse me, I want to let you in on a little secret. Red means you're suppose to hand over your phone number.

58. I want to let you in on a little secret. Green means go.

59. I like your tail (pause) lights.

60. Do you have as nice of curves as your car (assuming it's an Acura Integra, Toyota MR2, Ford Mustang, Mitsubushi Eclipse, or something of that sporty nature)?

    • If she says "no" I suggest that you keep on driving.

61. (To a girl driving Toyota, Honda, or other Asian car): Are you into Asian guys too or is it just the car?

62. If I was a police officer I would give you a ticket for being too hot. Instead I'm just going to ask that you hand over your phone number.

63. Do you need any maintenance?

    • You can follow this up with: "I know this restaurant/coffee shop down the road where I can check you out."

64. Are you high maintenance?

65. You can go as fast as you want over at my place.

66. The speed limit here is 35 mph (or whatever applies) but you can go as fast as you want on our date.

67. I think you found your "destiny-ation."

    • Obviously a spin on the word "destination."

68. Don't make me "love-rage" on you.

    - You can follow this up with: "I don't want to make you fall in love with me."
    - For those in the don't know: This is a spin on the word "roadrage."

69. Are you driving to the "Miss Universe" contest?

70. Did you know that every three months or so you should have your boyfriend changed?

    - You can follow this up with: "I'm offering a free boyfriend change today when one supplies a phone number."

71. The only danger on these streets is your beauty.

72. They should name a car after you: the "Beauty-ginni."

    - A humorous compliment based on the Lamborghini, one of the most luxurious sport cars in the world.

73. You didn't have to drive over, I would've picked you up.

74. Do you know if there is some chemistry around here?

    - If you say this pick-up line with a smile, you and the lady should have some chemistry of your own.
    - For those in the don't know: The word "chemistry" is synonymous with "love connection."

75. Dear Diary, I just met the girl of my dreams.

76. We could keep driving to Vegas and tie the knot. What do you think?

77. Don't hate me because I'm beautiful. But if you're going to hate me, then why don't you hit me with your phone number.

78. You know green doesn't mean go it means what's your phone number.

79. Did you carjack that ride from someone?

80. Gas makes the car go, but you make my heart go.

    - Some girls like extra cheese.

81. I just got tired of driving the Bentley.

    - This is works for maximum comedic value if you're driving a piece of crap.

82. The only thing that you are driving is me crazy.

83. Do you drive from Heaven every day?

84. What time are you do back to Heaven?

85. Can you tell me the quickest way to your heart?

Chapter 5
Classroom Pick-Up Lines

The classroom—regardless of whether it's high school, college, or post-college—has always been a great place to meet women. In this environment you are allotted more time to study the girl that you're interested in. You have more time to determine what type of girl she is (prude, flirt, slut) and what type of pick-up line she'll respond to most favorably.

The classroom has its advantages but beware of its disadvantages. If you hesitate too long you'll find some other guy moving in on your lady. Hesitation can be your worst enemy. Go get them!

1. I wish I could be the teacher for a day and have you paying attention to me.

2. What are you doing studying when you could be on the modeling runways for Gucci in Italy?

3. I saw you cheating on the test. Give me your phone number and I won't tell.

4. Is this "Human Sexuality 101?"

    - This works best when used during the first few days of class.

5. Hello! My name is Professor Porno, and I'll be your teacher today.

    - If she finds this amusing you can follow it up with: "My assistant is Mr. Ben Dover."

6. Is this "Hot Girls 101?"

    - This works best when used during the first few days of class.

7. I've got the best seat in the house. Have you ever thought about selling these seats?

8. I'm having a one-on-one study group tomorrow if you want to come.

9. Hello, I'm Professor Porno! Please take out your books and take off your clothes.

10. I'm trying to pay attention but you're so much more interesting.

11. You should teach a class called "How to be a Hot Girl."

12. Is this "How to Rob a Bank 101?"

    • This works best when used during the first few days of class.

13. Is this "Hot Girl in Your Class 101?"

    • This works best when used during the first few days of class.

14. I wasn't looking at your ass or anything but what kind of jeans are those?

15. You look confounded. Are you thinking about the class or asking me out?

16. Is this "College Sucks 101?"

    • This works best when used during the first few days of class.

17. I'm not as worried passing this test as I am passing yours.

18. Do you ever get distracted by your own hotness?

19. Studies show that if you study with me, it's good for your health.

20. I called and reserved that seat.

    • You can follow this up with: "I don't mind if we share it though."

21. Are you a cheater?

    • You can follow this up with: "How about in relationships?"
    • This line can lead to an interesting conversation about infidelity and divorce in America.

22. I heard you got in here on a beauty scholarship. Is that true?

23. If you let me look at your notes, I'll give you my phone number.

24. Did you know that I'm the coolest guy on campus?

25. That looks a lot like my book. Did you steal mine?

26. Are you majoring in "Breaking Guys Hearts?"

27. Hi, my name is whatever you want it to be.

28. What do you really want to do with your life?

   - Can lead to a provocative conversation about how everybody would rather be a rock star or actor/actress.

29. You should write your phone number down in your book in case you loose it and also so I can copy it down.

30. I just want to let you know that I don't go for every hot girl that chases me. If you want me, then you're going to have to show me something special.

   - Make her chase you. Build your ego, and they will come.

31. After class let's get lunch. Your treat. What do you say?

32. Are you registered for this class or are you just here to flirt with me?

33. I heard you're really not interested in this class but you just have a crush on the professor. Is this true?

   - This line can lead to a provocative conversation about dating people twice your age.

34. Hey, if you haven't noticed, I'm the hottest guy in the class.

   - Always give yourself props. If you don't give yourself compliments who will.

35. (Singing like Enrique Iglesias with his "Hero" song): I will be your hero baby.

36. I'm not making any guarantees here, but if you ask me, I'll probably give you my phone number.

37. You would be a lot happier in life if you quit paying attention in class and started paying more attention to me.

38. I'm willing to overlook your shortcomings and appreciate you for your faults as well as your good points.

39. Here's the deal! Let me know who you want to go out with in the class and I'll help you get your man. The catch is when you guys break up you have to go out with me.

40. Rumor has it that you're flunking this class. Is it true?

41. What kind of guys do you date?

    • No matter what she says, just say: "That's me!"

42. The only thing I can study in here is you.

43. The pop quiz today is: What's your phone number?

44. I didn't know this was the Supermodel Institute.

45. Are you taking notes or are you writing me a love letter?

46. Is this "Loser 101?"

    • This works best when used during the first few days of class.

47. I see you must have taken a class in "Perfect 101."

48. The nice thing about me is that I don't require a degree.

49. I'm offering a one-on-one class on dating if you're interested. It's an intensive six-week course and if you pass I'll be your boyfriend.

50. To pass my class you have to recite your phone number correctly.

51. Do you think you can teach me anything?

52. In forty-five minutes this class will be over but the memories of your beauty will last a lifetime. What do you think of my profound pondering?

53. What's it worth to you to take a look at my notes?

   • You can follow this up with: "I'm willing to take a kiss, your phone number, or a date."

54. Today I will be your teacher in numerology and our first lesson is the memorization of my phone number: 555-555-5555 (your phone number of course) and the recitation of your phone number.

55. What do you want to be when your grow up besides my girlfriend?

56. (To a girl in a math class): Excuse me, what's the square root/derivative of your hotness?

57. (To a girl in a history class): Tell me about the history of your love life?

58. (To a girl in a history class): Tell me about the history of your obsession with me.

   • Assume she's obsessed with you.

59. The only thing I'm learning in this class is how greatly distracting you are.

60. I can read you like a book. You come from…Mars (or the getto, North Pole, or some other crazy place). You like….M&Ms but only the blue ones because blue symbolizes peace (or Coke but hate Pepsi), and you only go out with guys that (describe yourself). Fuck me if I'm wrong but am I right?

   • You want to fill in the blanks with humorous comments whether or not they have any truth or not.

61. What's your test for prospective boyfriends?

   • No matter what she says you can follow it with: "I know I can ace it."

62. I think that I would pay more attention if you were teaching the class.

63. (To a girl who looks like she isn't paying attention): Are you getting a major in "I Don't Give A Shit?"

64. Tell me the truth! Is it hard to study with me in the class?

65. How come there's no "Class Clown 101?"

66. The great thing about me is that I don't charge tuition.

67. If you pay attention to me you might just learn something.

68. How come they don't have classes like "The History of Beer 101?"

69. Do you really remember anything that you've learned over the years?

    • This can lead to a provocative conversation about the futility of learning institutions.

70. I don't think the teacher knows what he's/she's talking about.

71. Do you prefer the pencil or the pen?

72. Do you prefer the backpack or the shoulder bag?

    • This can lead to a riveting conversation about the differences between backpack people vs. shoulder bag people.

73. What's a better profile of my face (turn your face from side to side)? My right side or my left side?

74. Would you mind waking me up when class is over?

75. I think they should have refreshment stands in class just like they have at the movie theater. What do you think?

76. If this was your class I would have no problem paying attention.

77. Do you know what time the love bell, I mean class bell rings?

78. Are you accepting resumes?

    • If she says "for what" you can say: "Your next boyfriend of course."

79. I'm studying for business, but what I really want to be when I grow up is your boyfriend.

80. (To a girl in a math class): According to my calculations, the more times I ask you out, the more likely you'll eventually go out with me. Is this calculation accurate?

81. Do you have "A"s, "B"s, "C"s, or "D"s?

    • Let the girl decide whether you're asking about her grades or her tits.

82. Are you the teacher's pet, class clown, or somewhere in between?

83. Would it be presumptuous for me to assume that you would let me cheat off of you?

84. General psychology says that the more you're exposed to something the more you like it. I figure that by the end of the quarter you should love me. What do you think?

85. Is now a bad time?

    • When she says "for what" you can say: "To begin our relationship."

86. Don't worry about getting your master's degree. You got the job. You can be my girlfriend.

87. Where do we go from here?

88. What chapter are you?

89. There's no book about me yet, you have to experience me first hand.

90. You can buy your books but you can't buy me lady.

91. I think dating you might be distracting to my learning, but I'm willing to overlook it.

92. You know you can take a lot of courses during your tenure here: psychology, sociology, biology. They're all fascinating but I highly suggest AllAboutMe.

93. Can I borrow your phone number for a second?

Chapter 6
Coffee Shop Pick-Up Lines

A coffee café is a very conductive environment for meeting women. A coffee cafe makes for a great pick-up environment because of its relaxed atmosphere and caffeinated beverages.

Caffeinated beverages give people a "lift," meaning that it makes them feel less drowsy and more mentally stimulated. This is good for you in that the girls you approach will be ready for your onslaught of mental bliss.

Most of the pick-up lines in this chapter were written specifically for Starbucks since that is the coffee franchise that dominates the landscape, however there are many lines that can be used at any coffee house or coffee-serving location. What are you waiting for? Go get them!

1. Do you have any idea what a Starbuck is?

    • Starbucks is the largest coffee franchise in the world and yet no one knows who or what a Starbuck is. She'll admire your inquisitiveness.

2. Do you know if they have hamburgers here?

    • She will smile at your ridiculous question.

3. Do you think they could make a hamburger out of coffee beans?

4. Doesn't the smell of coffee and hip-retro music want to make you fall in love?

    • This only applies if you're at a coffee cafe that plays hip-retro music.

5. Do you ever feel ripped off when you pay $1.50 for coffee?

6. Who is this Starbuck guy anyway?

7. I love a woman that can appreciate good coffee.

8. I never thought that I would meet the woman of my dreams at a coffee joint. Am I dreaming?

9. You look so cool sipping your coffee. Do you practice in the mirror at home?

10. How come none of these drinks are alcoholic?

11. Do you think Mr. Starbuck has a fetish for coffee?

12. Do you think Mr. Starbuck really drinks Sanka?

13. Would you hold it against me if I told you that you are hotter than this cup of coffee?

14. You're hotter than a McDonald's cup of coffee.

15. Did you come here for coffee or for me?

16. Are you on the menu?

17. Excuse me, I don't see you on the menu.

18. Let's see who can drink their coffee the fastest!

19. I apologize for being so distracting.

20. Something smells good! Is that your coffee or you?

21. Tell me the truth, what's hotter, that cup of coffee you're drinking or me?

22. What time should I pick you up tonight?

23. Are you going to finish that?

    • Whether you ask her this while she's drinking or when the coffee is at rest, just make sure you have a smile on so she thinks you're a cute flirt rather than a bum looking for a hand out.

24. How's the water and beans?

    • For those in the don't know: Coffee is made from water and ground beans.

25. Coffee must have happened by accident. Who would have thought that hot water and beans would be some great thing?

26. And then God said, let there be coffee.

27. How come Starbucks doesn't have value meals here? You know, like coffee and a muffin for $1.99?

28. I'm thinking about starting a franchise called Cheap Coffee. What do you think?

29. I'm thinking about starting a franchise called Cheaper Than Starbucks Coffee. What do you think?

30. Does your coffee get jealous of you being hotter?

31. Can you explain to me proper coffee etiquette?

32. Do you know if you can get reservations here?

33. If you want to conserve paper I can get a Grande and we can share.

34. Do you know if there is a VIP section here?

35. Do you think the coffee is actually better down in Columbia?

36. Have you read any good coffee books lately?

37. When you are through I would be honored to have your cup.

38. Do you think the people that work here get so addicted to coffee that they have to go to a Coffee Anonymous program so they can sleep again and de-brown their teeth?

39. Do you think if you irritate the workers here that they'll spit in your coffee?

40. What's your favorite thing about coffee?

41. How many coffee beans do you think went into making your tasty beverage?

42. I don't mean to sound presumptuous but do you think our kids will find it weird that we met in a coffee shop?

43. What do you think the chances are that the government owns Starbucks and they're putting mind-altering drugs into the coffee to manipulate our very existence?

44. Doesn't Starbuck sound like an ancient Roman god. Starbuck, god of coffee beans and stimulants?

45. Do you think Starbucks has a secret recipe like Coca-Cola and they keep it locked in a safe somewhere?

46. Would you go out with a guy that works at a coffee place if that was his only ambition in life?

47. What is your favorite thing about a hot cup of coffee?

48. Do you think Columbia is mad at Seattle for being the new mecca for coffee?

49. Do you think coffee will soon be like beer, with people growing beans locally and having micro-bean farms?

50. Excuse me, is it you or my coffee that's getting my heart rate up?

51. Tell me the truth, when you look for eligible bachelors in here do you look for the guys drinking the expensive coffee drinks?

52. You like coffee, I like coffee, what are the chances?

53. What's the largest cup of coffee that you've ever had?

54. I like my coffee like I like my women: hot and dark.

    • This is better used on a woman of color since it'll be seen as a compliment.

55. When I was a kid I thought coffee tasted like dirt and I still think it kind of does but I've gotten used to it. What do you think?

56. Don't you think coffee tastes like warmed up Coca-Cola without the sugar?

57. Do you think anybody has ever been married in a Starbucks?

58. I don't understand, Taco Bell has free refills, and this place charges 50 cents! What's up with that?

59. Is "coffee drinker" at the top of your list for things you look for in a man?

60. I don't know what a good tip at one these coffee places is? Ten cents? A quarter? Do you have any idea?

61. Do you think the people here deserve tips? At what point do you draw the line with tipping? Do you tip the guy at McDonald's too?

62. It's great to wake up with coffee but it's even better to wake up with ME.

63. (Singing like Enrique Iglesias in his "Hero" song): I can be your coffee baby.

    • She'll love your comedic spin on the hit song.

64. If your coffee isn't hot enough I'm sitting right over here.

65. If your coffee isn't strong enough I'm sitting right over here.

66. What do you think of the entrees here?

    • If she doesn't see your humor in calling the muffins and desserts entrees then simply tell her: "You know, the muffins and stuff."

67. How long have you been a coffee drinker?

68. Have you ever heard anyone burp at a Starbucks because I haven't?

    • This is best used on a younger woman who will find burping humor funny.

69. Have you ever wondered why the bathrooms at Starbucks are only built for one person? Weird.

70. Have you seen a waiter around here?

71. Where's the dancing in this place?

72. Starbucks was a great business name because "star" is synonymous with "big," and "bucks" is synonymous with "money," so Starbucks is really a secret name for "BigMoney." What do you think?

    • She'll love your ponderous mind.

73. There's an extra seat at my VIP table. Are you a very important person?

74. Are you a caffeine addict?

75. Here's a question. Why did Starbucks design one-person bathrooms when they're in the business of selling liquids?

76. If you were my girl I would never let you have some fifty-cent donut shop coffee.

77. Are you a coffee junkie?

78. Are you a professional coffee taster/drinker?

79. Have you noticed that they never play Metallica in here?

80. Do you think America has a coffee problem?

    • This line can lead to a provocative conversation about the proliferation of Starbucks coffee locations in America.

81. A person can go without water for three days but how long can a Starbucks junkie go without coffee?

82. Who do you think would be the best celebrity endorsement for Starbucks?

83. Do you think Jesus drank coffee?

84. Does coffee count for any of the major food groups?

85. Do you ever burn your coffee?

    • If she doesn't understand tell her: "Well your coffee is hot but you are steaming."

86. I can't make dinner but I can brew some pretty mean coffee.

87. Do you think the flagship Starbucks locations have valet parking?

88. 7-11 coffee isn't good enough for you huh?

89. What do you bet that Starbucks comes out with their own magazine pretty soon?

Chapter 7
Crazy-Stupid Pick-Up Lines

Crazy-Stupid Pick-Up Lines are great because they pose ridiculous questions that lead to ridiculous conversations. These are subtle pick-up lines that masquerade as silly questions. These pick-up lines are perfect if you aren't feeling aggressive.

Just like Anytime Pick-Up Lines these lines can be used anywhere. Go get them!

1. Do you think if Britney Spears was a transsexual people would still buy her records?

2. Do you think Arnold Schwarzenegger is really a cyborg?

3. Did you hear that beer causes cancer?

    - Once she spits out her beer in shock you can tell her "just kidding" for a little comic relief.

4. Did you hear Brad Pitt is giving up acting and he's doing a rap album with Shaquille O'Neil?

    - When she gets done puking you can tell her "just kidding" for a little comic relief.

5. Who do you think would win in a fight: Tom Brokaw or Peter Jennings?

6. Who do you think would win in a fight: Pink or Christina Aguilera?

7. Who do you think would win in a fight: Oprah or Rosie O'Donnell?

8. Who do you think would win in a fight: The kid from "The Sixth Sense" or the kid from "Jerry Maguire?"

9. Who do you think would win in a fight: Mary-Kate Olsen or Ashley Olsen?

10. Who do you think would win in a fight: Jesus or Buddha?

11. Who do you think would win in a fight: Eminem or Vanilla Ice?

12. Who do you think would win in a fight: Clay Aiken or Lance from NSYNC?

13. Who do you think would win in a fight: Mike Tyson or an average guy with a gun?

14. Who do you think would win in a fight: Mr. T or Arnold Schwarzenegger?

15. Who do you think would win in a fight: Queen Latifah or the singer from Creed?

16. Who would you be more embarrassed to date: a guy that lives with his parents or a guy that drives a Ford Aspire?

17. Who would you be more embarrassed to date: a male nurse or a male make-up artist?

18. Who would you be more embarrassed to date: a guy that works at Burger King or a guy that works at McDonald's?

19. Who would you be more embarrassed to date: a horrible dresser or a guy that stinks?

20. Who would you more embarrassed to date: a bus boy or a newspaper delivery guy?

21. Who would you be more embarrassed to date: a super skinny guy or a super fat guy?

22. Who would you be more embarrassed to date: a proctologist or a urologist?

    • For those in the don't know: A proctologist is a doctor who specializes in the anus and an urologist is a doctor who specializes in the penis.

23. What's the oldest guy that you would date? Why?

24. What's the youngest guy that you would date? Why?

25. Do you think if beer wasn't alcoholic that people would still drink it?

26. If they run out of towels in the restroom feel free to dry your hands off on me.

27. The Whopper or the Big Mac, which is better? Why?

28. Coke or Pepsi, which is better? Why?

29. Who do you think is hotter: me or that guy over there?

30. What makes you more special than the rest of the girls in here?

31. I'll be your man agent tonight, but I get ten percent of all future gifts and money that he gives you.

32. I'll be your man agent tonight, but I get ten percent of all future bootie that they get.

33. Will you be my pimp?

34. Tell me the truth, do you drink just to look cool?

35. Tell me the truth, do you smoke just to look cool?

36. Have you been drinking all day or did you just start?

37. I may not be attractive to you now, but check me out after you've had a few more.

38. Is it possible for such a strong attraction to be one sided? I mean think of two magnets, there is mutual force going on there.

39. (Show her your hand): Do you think I have what it takes to be a hand model?

40. (Spin around and start fiddling with your jacket): Can you help me with my jacket?

    - This is a play on role reversal. If she is a lady she will help you remove your jacket. If you succeed in getting her assistance, congratulations! You got her to touch you first and that's always an accomplishment.

41. If you take advantage of me, I won't tell anyone about it.

42. Where do we do from here?

43. Here's the deal: I'll let you know when guys are checking you out and you let me know when girls are checking me out. What do you think?

44. Can you do me a favor and let me know when girls are checking me out?

45. In baseball you have three strikes until your out, three outs in an inning, and nine innings until the game is over. Is it OK if we approach me picking up on you like that?

46. I'm looking for an intern for my love life. Are you interested?

47. Do you have a license for that beauty?

48. You can look but you can't touch.

49. Do you like a man with a hairy chest or smooth chest?

50. I don't know if it's lust or love but I definitely feel something for you.

51. Be honest, if you could have multiple husbands legally and they were cool with it, do you think you would take that option?

52. Do you need me to kick any jerk's ass around here?

53. You name it and you got it: a beer, hug, kiss, grope, whatever you want.

54. What time should I get you up tomorrow morning?

55. The deal is you pay for a taxi and cook me breakfast in the morning.

56. (Point at some random girl in the distance): That girl over there said you don't have what it takes to get me in the sack.

57. They used to say "Make Love Not War" in the 1970s and I don't have a problem with that. What do you say you and I support this old but still relevant hippie slogan and make some love?

58. I know we can work through whatever problems that we might encounter.

59. Do you think you're worthy?

60. If you have ever wondered what your purpose on earth was, well I'm here.

61. Your wait is over.

    • If she says "what wait" you can follow up with: "The wait for the man of your dreams. I'm here."

62. Can you pat your head and rub your tummy at the same time?

    • After she does it or says "yes" you can follow up with: "Good. How about kissing me while grabbing my butt?"

63. I have a clothing removal business and the first time is free.

64. How old were you when you realized you liked boys?

65. I've been bad, would you mind spanking me?

66. What's your name, Perfect?

67. What's it like being a girl?

68. Was that you calling my name over here?

69. (Whispering "The Sixth Sense" style): I see beautiful people.

70. Your parents must have paid off God pretty good.

71. I always wondered what would happen if two supermodels mated.

72. Are you just going to sit there, or are you going to ask me out?

73. Happy hour is over but not my horny hour.

74. Happy hour may be over but you can maintain the happiness by taking body shots off my bootie.

75. My arms are paralyzed, do you think you can get my wallet for me?

    • Sometimes you have to tell a little white lie to get a girl to touch your butt.

76. If it's money you're after, I consider McDonald's fine dining.

    • This is a great way to filter out the gold diggers.

77. Have you seen my confidence around here?

78. What's worse: a man with thinning hair or a twenty-pound beer gut?

    • Can lead to a provocative conversation about beauty and aging.

79. What do you think my best feature is?

    • To add some humor to this, spin around and shake your ass a little.

80. Have you seen my sense of humor around here?

    • If you hear someone laugh you can follow it up with: "I think that guy/girl stole it."

81. Have you driven a Ford lately?

    • For those in the don't know: "Have you driven a Ford lately" is Ford's marketing slogan.

    • Can lead to a riveting conversation about the evolution of the Ford Mustang or the Ford Explorer tire explosion tragedies.

82. Do you find my strikingly handsome or boldly beautiful?

83. Who do you think would win in a fight: Clint Eastwood or Queen Latifah?

84. Who do you think would win in a fight: Justin Timberlake or Pink?

85. The results are in! I'm the best catch in here. The results were handled by an independent poll handled by me.

86. Which pant leg do you address first: the right or the left?

87. Do you hang up on telemarketers or do you threaten them?

88. Did you just break up from a long relationship and just want to have fun now?

89. I'm not a doctor, but I like to play the game.

90. If you aren't interested, possibly you know someone who is?

91. If things don't work with your top picks tonight, I'll be over here waiting patiently.

92. Who would win in a fight: Gary Coleman or Mini-Me?

93. They say a woman's profile resembles the letter "S." What letter do you think a man's profile represents?

94. I'm collecting donations for my Ferrari fund tonight if you're feeling generous.

95. If size matters, I'm not Chinese.

96. If size matters, I'm one quarter black.

97. Boxers or briefs?

98. Do I make you horny baby?

   • You can follow this up with: "Did you know Austin Powers stole that line from me."

Chapter 8
Dance Club Pick-Up Lines

The dance club has always been a stupendous environment to meet women due to its erotic nature: sexy outfits, erotic beats, and the close proximity of people. This is an atmosphere where if you carefully select the right elements of PJCSP you can be making out on the dance floor in no time. Go get them!

1. It's so hard to hear in here, do you just want to make out?

2. Rumor has it that you look good, but you can't dance. Is this true?

   • She'll want to prove to you that she can.

3. If you think my looks are good, you have to check out my dancing.

4. Are you a professional, "dancer" that is?

   • For those in the don't know: A professional or "pro" is synonymous with prostitute.

5. Does your hotness get in the way of your dancing?

6. How about a trade? I'll give you compliments and you give me dance lessons?

7. (Dancing with a girl): If you just want to dance in your bra, I won't hold it against you.

8. Do you like to dance horizontally?

   • For those in the don't know: To "dance horizontally" is synonymous with "fucking."

9. I just want to let you know that when we go out there and dance and you see my moves, I'm not gay, I'm just a damn good dancer.

10. So when is your album coming out?

   • For those in the don't know: Many pop stars started their careers as dancers including Madonna, J-Lo, Bobby Brown, P-Ditty, and others.

11. Where are your back up dancers at?

12. I saw your moves out there. Are you signing autographs?

13. I saw your moves out there and the dance floor will never be the same again.

14. I saw your moves out there and you need to head over to Dance USA.

15. Would it be presumptuous to assume that you were dancing for me out there?

16. Are you here to have fun or are you here to try out for FAME?

17. Try to see me as a human being and not just a piece of meat.

18. Are you good at lap dances too?

   • Best used on a girl that looks a little on the wild side.

19. I know this French dance but it's with the tongues.

20. I can't be one-hundred percent, but from the dance floor it appeared that you were checking me out.

21. Are you a cyborg sent from the future to seduce me?

   • References to "The Terminator" movie are always good for a quick giggle.

22. Do you do any of that Madonna vogue stuff? (At the end of the question start to vogue for maximum comedic value. If you're not familiar with the vogue dance try downloading the "Vogue" video from the Internet.)

23. You know I totally can identify with what Sisqo is singing about in the "Thong Song."

   • Works for maximum comedic value if she's wearing a thong.

24. May I have this dance, and the next one, and the next one, and the next one, and the next one?

25. You won't need X if I'm around.

26. What song is better to shake your ass to: Mystikal's "Shake Your Ass" or Rex N Effect's "Rumpshaker?"

27. What song do you think is better to jump to: Kris Kros's "Jump" or House of Pain's "Jump Around?"

28. I know this great naked dance. It's called "Fucking."

29. I don't want to brag, but I know how to do the Macarena.

30. I was wondering if you would like to make "Dirty Dancing 4?"

31. What other things do you think dancing is similar to?

32. How come animals don't dance?

33. Do you think Adam and Eve danced?

34. I'm offering free slow dance lessons tonight if you want to learn.

35. My favorite dance is the lap dance. What about yours?

36. Do you know the lap dance?

37. May I have this lap dance?

38. What ever happened to square dancing?

39. Do you think M.C. Hammer's wife even tries to keep up with him?

40. Do you think the character in "Footloose" was a closet homosexual?

   • For those in the don't know: "Footloose" was a movie about a heterosexual man who danced around like a girl.

41. You know dancing has gotten so dirty these days that in another twenty years they may just call it fucking.

42. I learned my rhythm from another activity similar to dancing.

43. Do you know anybody who bought that "Lord Of The Dance" video?

44. Have you ever considered what would happen if Richard Simmons and the Lord of the Dance got together and figured out how to procreate?

    • For those in the don't know: Richard Simmons was a gay exercise guru in the 1980s that sported a huge white (as in Caucasian) Afro and was best known for his exercise video "Sweating to the Oldies." The Lord of the Dance was an effeminate tap dancer that headed up a huge tap production called "The Lord of the Dance" that was made available in late-night infomercials.

45. Do you know if they do the Hokey Pokey here?

    • For those in the don't know: The Hokey Pokey is the bastard father of the Macarena.

46. I'm having a "Shake It" contest tonight and you're up.

    • You can follow this up with: "The winner gets my phone number."

47. If you can out dance me, I'll give you my phone number.

48. Hey if you give me your phone number, I'll go out to the dance floor and shake it like a salt shaker.

49. There's a pole dancing contest tonight. I'm the pole and the winner gets my phone number. Are you in?

50. I'm opening up a club in my bedroom tonight and it's called Club You.

51. I just want to let you know that I make out a lot better than I dance.

52. So when is your dance-off with Britney Spears?

53. You know those Macarena guys stole my moves.

54. I used to have moves, but Justin Timberlake bought them off me and I vowed never to use them again.

55. I can't dance very well but I can jump when those "jump jump" songs come on.

56. How come God gave gay guys all the good dance moves?

57. Your dancing makes me want to be a better person.

58. Next time you can save the five dollars (or whatever the club cover was) by coming over to my place and I'll turn up the music real loud and turn the lights on and off. What do you think?

59. Excuse me, can you tell me where the dance floor is?

    • For maximum comedic value, use this when the dance floor is right in front of your face.

60. Do you know the tongue dance?

    • If she seems receptive then go for the kiss.

61. Hey I can't dance but I'll go out there, watch you, and clap my hands in approval.

62. The moves I've been working on aren't on the dance floor, they're on the bedroom floor.

63. Does your Dad know that you dance like that?

64. What's your top A.J.P.H., that's Ass Jiggle Per Hour?

65. I see your dancing skills are stellar. What else are you good at?

66. If you want to know the truth, I can't dance, but I do have a job and a car.

67. Rumor has it that you really want to enter my kissing contest but you're too chicken shit.

68. Who do you think is a better dancer: M.C. Hammer or Michael Jackson?

69. Do you relate more to a ballerina or a stripper when you dance?

70. You have more moves than a U-Haul truck.

71. I challenge you to a dance-off!

72. What happens when the music stops?

73. I don't know who has more rhythm: you or the music?

74. Does Britney Spears know that you stole her moves?

75. If you were a record I would spin you constantly.

76. Did you escape from a Britney Spears video?

77. Are you trying to hyptomize me into a love trance with your dance moves?

78. If you need a beat to step to, just listen to my heart.

79. My heartbeat has better rhythm than this song.

80. Were you in that movie "Dirty Dancing?"

81. Are you the Lady Lord of the Dance?

82. Did you steal those moves?

83. I don't know if you were showing off out there but I'm impressed.

84. Did you go to the MC Hammer Academy?

85. Did you train with Vanilla Ice?

86. You know what's better than E? ME!

87. Did you think the movie "Dirty Dancing" was really that dirty?

88. What's broken with break dancing anyway?

89. You have more moves than a vagabond.

    • For those in the don't know: A vagabond is a person, usually without a permanent home, that wonders from place to place.

90. (If you're not Afro-American): Do you have any idea why Afro-Americans are better dancers than the rest of us?

91. My dance floor moves are OK but give me a strip pole and I really come alive.

Chapter 9
Grocery Store Pick-Up Lines

The grocery store is often a neglected location when it comes to picking up women. Food is very erotic in the sense that it's eaten with the mouth and it's shaped like many erotic body parts. These sensual relationships definitely sit upon the subconscious of the female mind.

You'll be surprised with the receptivity of women in grocery stores who are used to cowardly men pushing their shopping carts around like scared little girls. Go get them!

1. (Holding up a piece of fruit): Do you know how to squeeze these things to tell if they're ripe?

2. Do you know if they're sampling anything in here today?

    • If she says "no" you can say: "Well I'm giving out free smiles today."

3. I thought you might want to know that checker number five is really slow.

4. You look like a champion, do you eat Wheaties?

    • For those in the don't know: Wheaties is a breakfast cereal whose slogan is "The Breakfast of Champions."

5. My club card is the only thing that keeps me going in this crazy world.

6. (At Ralph's Grocery Chain): Have you seen Ralph?

7. How do you make the decision between paper and plastic?

8. I love the carts at this store. Good wheels, nice steering.

9. If you were given a three-minute shopping spree in here, what would be your strategy?

10. I've been eating Wheaties my whole life and I'm still not a champion. Do you think I should sue?

11. Do you think Del Giorno's Pizza is better than delivery?

    • For those in the don't know: Del Giorno's Pizza's marketing slogan is: "It's not delivery, it's Del Giorno." They are making an attempt to say that their home-baked pizza is better than delivery.

12. Do you think The Rice Crispy Guys, Captain Crunch, and Lucky Charm all hang out together?

13. Have you seen my grocery cart around here?

14. (Look in a girl's cart, see what groceries she has, get the same, and then proceed): Hey you like milk (or whatever the item is) too? I thought I was the only one.

15. (With a coupon in your hand): I'll give you this coupon if you give me your phone number.

16. What's cooking?

17. Do you know where the whip cream section is?

    • For those in the don't know: Whip cream is often a favorite sex food.

18. So, what's for dinner?

19. So, are you cooking tonight?

20. What time is dinner?

21. Should I bring dessert?

22. Do you want to take a ride in my cart?

    • If she is receptive then give her a ride.

23. Have you seen my new cart?

24. I think I have a faster cart than yours.

25. (Bump your cart into girl's cart): I'm sorry, my cart's brakes are bad.

26. (When you are by the carrots): How are you supposed to choose carrots?

   • For those in the don't know: Carrots and cucumbers are the two vegetables most commonly associated with men's penises.

27. I heard they have good cucumbers here. Is this true?

28. (Point at her cart): Do you have a license to drive that thing?

29. (In line together): Is it on you tonight?

30. Are you going to pay for that stuff or are you going to stuff it all into your clothes and steal it?

31. Do you know what isle the extra-large condemns are on?

32. Do you know if they sell Playboy here?

   • If she seems offended tell her: "I only read it for the excellent journalism."

33. You think 8:00 p.m. is good?

   • When she says "good for what" you can say: "A good time for you to be at my place for dinner tonight."

34. I can't make any food but I can make you sweat.

   • This is best used on a female that is looking a little frisky.

35. (To a skinny girl with a full cart): Are you eating all that tonight?

   • Say this to a skinny girl and she'll admire your comedic wit however if say this to a fat girl she'll probably slap you silly.

36. (Pointing at a girl's cart): It's just like driving a car, the slow lane is on the right, and the fast lane is on the left, and only pass if you can avoid a collision.

37. I'm available for dinner at $6.75 an hour and that includes provocative conversation.

38. Are you going to buy that stuff or do you just like pushing carts around with food in them?

39. So, how long have you been shopping for groceries?

40. Do you know if they have maps here so you can actually find the stuff you're looking for?

41. Will you give me a ride in your cart?

42. How much for you to push me around in your cart and grab the stuff that I need?

43. Don't you think they should make people take a class in grocery cart etiquette because you always get some jackass that leaves their cart right in the middle of the isle?

44. They always ask you "paper or plastic." Do you think they will let you have "paper and plastic?"

45. Do you think the checkers and stockers here get hungry more often than other people whom are always working around food?

46. (If you have a case of pop in your basket): Do you know if a case of pop is one item or twenty-four items because I'm trying to decide which line to get in here?

47. If I wrote a book called *How to Choose a Grocery Line* would you buy it?

48. What's worse in a grocery line: an old person or a person with a bunch of coupons?

49. (In the fruit or vegetable section): Do I look ripe?

50. (In the fruit or vegetable section): Are you ripe for a new love interest?

51. (Pointing to your ass while in the fruit or vegetable section): Does this look ripe to you?

52. Do you take coupons?

53. Do you know where the breasts are, the chicken breasts?

54. I can't find the dessert section, can I have you instead?

55. I have this great recipe called "Attraction." The ingredients are you and me.

56. My expiration date is next week so you better use me soon.

57. What's your expiration date, because I wouldn't want you to go to waste?

58. I'm the best deal in here because I have no expiration date.

59. Do you know where I can find some sugar around here?

   - For those in the don't know: Sugar is synonymous with love and affection.

60. Can you tell me what ingredients I need to make YOU?

61. The best deal in here is ME and you don't need any coupons.

62. Aren't you surprised there aren't more cart accidents in here?

63. How come they don't have horns on these carts?

64. Why do they make these carts so big? You rarely ever see anybody with a full cart!

65. I think they should have three sizes of carts in here: single, couple, and Catholic.

66. What's sweeter: Krispy Crème Donuts or you?

67. What's the deal with everybody wanting this food stuff?

68. Coke or Pepsi? Which is better?

   - This is one of the greatest philosophical questions of all time.

69. Do you know any recipes for a good time?

70. Are you giving out free samples today?

71. What isle are you on?

72. Do you know if they have any coupons for your phone number?

73. Have you heard of the new ME dessert?

74. You know they have some great dinners here, but nothing beats dinner at my place.

75. In case you're interested, I'm running a free bed and breakfast.

76. Have you thought about getting a new cart?

77. Is that your grocery cart or did you bring your own from home?

78. I can't tell, are you ripe?

79. You make me hungry.

80. Do you know if Ding Dongs expire?

81. What do you do with your milk when it's past the expiration date?

82. How's the steering alignment on your cart?

83. If all the lines are pretty equal how do you know which one to go with?

84. Which line is worse: the line with two old people or a slow checker?

85. Which line is worse: a line with two old people or a checker with no bagger?

86. What happens if you get in the "ten items or less line" and you have eleven items?

87. Am I on your list?

   • This is most effective when a girl is looking at her grocery list.

Chapter 10
Gym Pick-Up Lines

Revealing clothes, sexy bodies, and copious sweat make the gym an ideal place to pick up women. Most men fail at meeting girls at the gym because they get too caught up in looking at the shapely beauties. Looking is for the rookies. With over eighty Gym Pick-Up Lines it's time to step up to the big leagues and start talking. Go get them!

1. Don't you hate it when the guys check you out all the time? Me too.

2. I can't find the other five-hundred pound weight. Have you seen it around here?

    • This works for maximum comedic value if you don't look like you can lift five-hundred pounds.

3. Why is it that there are more guys at the gym than girls?

4. Have you noticed that guys seem more concerned about their bodies these days than women?

    • This line can lead to a provocative conversation about vanity and the evolution of sexy bodies in society.

5. Did you know that the Surgeon General came out with a new study that says working out is bad for you? Just kidding.

6. Have you ever noticed that most the people here never get in better shape. Why is that?

    • This line can lead to a provocative conversation about how most people lack discipline in their lives.

7. Can you smoke in here? Just kidding.

. Did you used to be really fat? There was this person that looked just like you a year ago but she was a hundred pounds heavier.

   • This works best on a thin girl who looks like she's never been fat.

. Can you tell me in a week if I look any more attractive?

0. Which do you think is hotter: having a lean-toned body or a beefed-out-Schwarzenegger body?

1. Do you know if those ab machines work?

   • Can lead to a provocative conversation about late-night infomercials.

2. (To a girl on a treadmill): Who are you running from?

3. (To a girl on a treadmill): I think it's going to take you awhile to get there.

4. (To a girl on a treadmill): You're not going anywhere.

   • Sometimes playing stupid is funny to women.

5. (To a girl on a Stairmaster): Is the elevator broke?

6. (To a girl on a Stairmaster): Is there room on there for two?

7. Do you have a work out video of your own?

8. You know some people don't look so hot when they work out but you look hotter.

9. Atkins? Weight Watchers? Jenny Craig? What's your secret?

0. What do you think of my man boobs?

   • It doesn't matter if you have rock-hard pecs or saggy bags for a chest, the fact that you refer to your chest as "man boobs" will put a smile on her face.

1. (To a girl who is working out): I think you could go harder.

2. (To a girl lifting a weight or on a machine): Is that all you got?

3. I'm all real, no implants.

24. I don't have a visible boxer line do I?

   - For those in the don't know: Girls are always concerned whether they're showing a visible panty line, and this is a comedic twist on that concern.

25. I'll be your personal trainer, I just don't know much about fitness.

26. If you need a massage after you work out, I'm an amateur masseuse.

27. Is that a real six pack or is that an implant?

28. Do you think my six pack is real or an implant?

29. What do you think of guys that get muscle implants?

30. If there is ever a line at the drinking fountain, you can cut right in front of me.

31. Do you teach any classes here?

32. Do they have pizza and beer here? Just kidding.

33. Is working out supposed to be fun?

34. I've noticed some guys here grunt when they work out and other guys don't. Do you have any idea what that is about?

35. What do you think is more important on a man: his triceps or biceps?

36. (Point at your water): If you need some water I'm selling it for $1.00 a sip.

37. (Point at your towel): If you need a towel I'm selling mine for a $1.00 a wipe.

38. I had this dream that I was at the gym and you were flirting with me. What do you think this means?

   - This line can lead to a provocative conversation about dream interpretation.

39. Have you seen Richard Simmons around here?

   - For those in the don't know: Richard Simmons was a work out guru of the 1980s who was best known for his huge afro and gay tendencies including short shorts and loose tank tops.

40. Are you here for an exercise book signing?

   - If she seems confused just tell her: "You just look in such good shape I figured you had to have your own exercise book."

41. Do you think anybody has ever used that Tai Bo workout stuff to kick anybody's ass?

42. Have you ever met anyone at the gym before?

43. If you aren't finished by closing time, you can finish at my place.

44. Do you think it's appropriate for men to wear spandex at the gym?

45. Why do you think they make men wear shirts at the gym?

46. (To a girl on a workout machine): I wish I was your machine.

47. Did you know that it's better to listen to high tempo music when you're working out because your body becomes entrained with the music and you have a more intense workout.

   - This is an actual workout tip.

48. Have you seen a waitress around here?

49. Right now the only magazine cover I could be on would be called *Dough Boy*.

50. (At 24 HR Fitness): What do you think about those Bally Total Fitness people?

51. (At Bally Total Fitness): What do you think about those 24 HR Fitness people?

52. Do you really like being here or is it a pain in the ass for you?

53. Would you get one of those Extreme Makeovers if it was given to you?

   - For those in the don't know: "Extreme Makeover" is a reality television show that provides numerous cosmetic surgeries to improve some average joe's/jane's physical attributes: nosejobs, boobjobs, lipjobs, hairjobs, teethjobs, etc.

54. Would you hold it against me if I told you that all my muscles were implants?

55. You know being fat in the old days was a sign of prosperity, status, and marriage eligibility. Do you think that will come back in style any time soon?

56. (You struggling with a weight and a girl passing by): Can you give me a hand with this?

57. Don't you think they should have certain days that the sweaty people who soak the machines are able to come in and other days when they lock them out?

58. Someone told me the real way to lose weight is not working out but to quit eating like a pig. Do you think that's true?

59. (If you're a skinny guy): I don't understand why Kate Moss is considered perfect and I'm not. Where's my seven-figure modeling contract?

60. Excuse me, if you see me running on the treadmill can you let me know if I look cool or not? I don't want to look like a moron.

   • Can lead to a riveting conversation about people's workout faces.

61. Is being healthy all it's cracked up to be?

62. There's a lot of weight around here: my weight, your weight, that guy's weight, and all the weights.

63. I'm confused. Is it calories, carbs, or is it all bull crap?

64. (To a girl on a workout machine): Wow, you're gong to make that machine tired.

65. I know a great treat with zero calories. ME!

66. What's your nutritional content?

67. Excuse me, is your name Solid?

68. Excuse me, is your name Nonfat?

69. (Point at your arms): Don't worry, these guns are on safety.

    - For those in the don't know: Arm muscles on men are commonly referred to by men as "guns."

70. They didn't tell me about you when they were selling me the membership.

71. Do you think the guy who designed that Bowflex machine on television was an archer?

72. Do you think Arnold Schwarzenegger is still on steroids?

73. Are you a good work out?

74. Here's a secret for you, tunafish at night. Zero carbs, zero fat.

    - This is an actual health tip for those that are looking to loose weight.

75. Have you seen my concentration around here?

76. Don't you create a fire hazard for this place?

77. If I was your parents I would be proud.

78. How's the drinking fountain here?

79. Your parents must be beautiful.

80. Are you warming that machine up for me?

81. Think you can lift me?

82. Are you the prize for any contests here?

Chapter 11
Internet Pick-Up Lines

The Internet is the latest rage when it comes to meeting women. On the positive side it's great because you don't even have to leave the house to meet them. On the negative side you don't always know exactly what you're getting.

Your pick-up strategy will be a little bit different for the Internet. Rushing through PJCSP won't be your best interest in this environment. Relationships on the Internet tend to blossom after a succession of private chat room conversations or emails. The elements of the PJCSP pick-up formula will work for you in this environment but you'll want to hold off on attaining the phone number until you've had a few Internet encounters to win her trust and affection.

There are thousands of great date websites out there for you to explore. If you haven't dove into this terrain yet, check out the most popular ones below. Go get them!

www.match.com : Match.com is the most popular dating service on the Internet with profiles numbering in the millions. Their website claims that over 89,000 people in 2003 found the person that they were looking for.

www.friendster.com : Friendster.com is a meeting place in which all the profiles available for view are related to your circle of friends whether it's one degree of separation or six. It's a fascinating website and at the present time it's free.

http://chat.yahoo.com/ : There are chat rooms on most I.S.P.s (Internet Service Providers) and some search engines such as yahoo. Here you can chat live with people in your city or people all the way across the world. This service is free.

www.adultfriendfinder.com : This site claims to be the largest sex and swinger personals site with over six million members.

1. I just want to let you know, I don't chat with just any girl.

2. Tell me the truth, does my fast (or slow) typing turn you on?

3. The speed and accuracy of your typing is so sexy.

4. I wish I was your keyboard.

5. I'm going to sneak into your heart fast like a pop-up ad.

6. Love at first chat.

    For those in the don't know: This is a spin off the famous phrase: "Love at first sight."

7. If size matters I can use a bigger font.

8. Is that a fake picture, or are you really that fine?

    • It has been known that no one online ever looks as good as their picture.

9. You're so cool, that even if you've put on fifty pounds since your picture, I won't care.

10. You're not really a dude are you?

11. All you are to me is a bunch or words.

12. What's your w.p.m. (words per minute)?

    • You can follow this up with: "What's your t.o.m.p.m. (thoughts of me per minute)?"

13. Friendster is cool but what about Sexster, wouldn't that be cooler?

14. When are you going to get a web cam so I can see you shake it?

15. Quit web surfing and surf me instead.

16. I wish we could meet in cyberspace so we could make out.

17. Excuse me, do my words make you hot?

18. Do you have any viruses, computer viruses that is?

19. What would you do if you found out that I was a program?

- This line can lead to a provocative conversation that addresses the question posed in the movie "A.I.": Can man love a machine?

20. Would it matter if I was really a big fat wookie of a man?

21. Would you hold it against me if my w.p.m. is only five and a half?

- A girl might find these hilarious if she catches the sexual implications of the question. The average man's penis is five and a half inches long.

    NOTE: Some studies say six inches.

22. Think of the ugliest guy possible so that when we finally meet I'll be hot.

23. Are you a nerd?

- Some girls like bullies and jerks.

24. I wish I could download you.

25. If you were a file I wouldn't share you with anybody.

26. How big is your monitors?

- The grammatical error here is on purpose because by saying monitors instead of monitor you are humorously hinting at her tits.

27. Typing is not the only thing that I'm good at.

28. I've got the hardware, do you have the software?

29. I see your good at typing, what else are you good at?

30. I use my hands to type but I use them for other things too.

31. Are you jealous of my mouse?

32. Would it be too much to ask you for a jpeg of you stripping?

33. Describe your software?

    • Let her decide whether you're talking about programs or her body. Most likely she'll tell you about her programs. When she finishes you can follow up with: "What about your other software?"

34. If you were a program, you would be called *Beautiful.*

35. If you were a program, you would be called *Addiction.*

36. If you were a program, you would be called *Trouble.*

37. Are you a hacker, because you're breaking into my heart?

38. Do you take Pay Pal?

39. I'm a hacker, but it's not your files that you should worry about but your heart.

40. Do you like a lot of RAM?

    • For those in the don't know: RAM stands for Random Access Memory. It can also be interpreted as a sexual innuendo, depending on the girl.

41. You should be called X, because you're making me love-crazy.

42. You better check the time, so you remember exactly the moment that you fell in love.

43. I want you to look at me like you look at your monitor, and hold me like you hold your mouse.

44. You can call me your I.L.P., your Internet Love Provider.

45. You make me chat like I've never chatted before.

46. I would love you even if you were a pop-up ad.

47. What kind of hardware do you like?

    • For those in the don't know: "Hardware" is a sexual innuendo for "dick."

48. I don't pay for my software, I get it for free.

    - You can follow this up with: "I'm not talking about programs."

49. If you were mine I would never put you on Ebay.

50. I wanted to put my love on Ebay but I couldn't because it's priceless.

51. I have enough Friendsters, I'm looking for a Lovester.

52. Chat dirty to me.

    - For those in the don't know: This is a comedic twist on the famous phrase, "Talk dirty to me."

53. If this relationship is really going to work, you're going to have to email me a picture of you naked.

54. If you turn on your web cam and dance naked for me I won't hold it against you.

55. If you were a website you would be www. Beautiful.com.

56. So when can we go from cyberspace to my place?

57. Do you know how to get from cyberspace to first base?

58. If I was using yahoo to search for you what search terms would I use?

59. If you were a baseball game what would be your title: *First Base, Second Base, Third Base, Home Run,* or *Grand Slam*?

    - For those in the don't know: This pick-up line is based on the male/female sexual contact baseball analogy where first base equals kissing, second base equals feeling the goods, third base equals oral sex, home run equals fucking, and grand slam equals you and her three friends.

60. I want to click your mouse.

61. Would it be ok if I Ask Jeeves how many guys you've been with?

    - For those in the don't know: AskJeeves.com is a search engine that masquerades as a butler.

62. I can see by your typing that you like to take things slow.

63. Are you into hardware and/or software?

    • This is a great way to comically explore whether she's bisexual.

64. I'm trying to write a program for you to fall in love with me.

65. I will be your keyboard baby.

    • This is a riff off of the Enrique Iglesias song "Hero" which has a chorus of "I can be your hero baby."

66. I'm pretty adventurous. I'm into surfing, web surfing that is.

67. I have the hardware if you have the software.

68. I don't stalk my ex-girlfriends, I just spam them.

69. Ask Geeves was like my surrogate father.

    • For those in the don't know: Surrogate is a person appointed to act for another, a substitute.

70. I know you've web surfed before but have you ever man surfed?

71. Does AOL stand of Another Online Loser?

    • She'll love your sarcasm.

72. What's your download time?

73. How long it takes you to download me is all up to you.

    • Some say "download" is a sexual innuendo for "sex."

74. How old were you when you got your first piece of hardware?

75. I got my first piece of software when I was thirteen.

76. Do you like your men with dial up or cable?

77. How come the search engines all have crazy names: Yahoo, Google, Alta Vista?

78. Have you ever bid for a boyfriend on Ebay?

79. Do you have anything in your mouth right now?

    - Sometimes it's good to find out up front if she has an oral fixation.

80. Wouldn't it be funny if they had a website like Friendster, called Sexter, so you could see whom everybody has slept with?

81. I like my women like I like my search engines: fast and efficient.

82. Are you really this amazing, or are you just one of those guys working for a porn site posing as a great girl to lure me to a porn site to steal my hard earned money?

83. How many I.S.P.s have you had?

    - This hints at the sensitive question: how many partners have you had?

84. I like to take things slow, like the download time of a graphic intense, flash built website with dial up.

    - She'll love your Internet analogy.

85. Be honest, when was the last time you looked as good as you look in your picture?

86. What's your best piece of software?

87. What's the best piece of hardware that you've ever had?

88. When you think of your ideal man, does he surf for porn on the Internet?

89. I would switch I.S.P.s for you.

90. You could never be sold on Ebay because you're priceless.

91. I bet if I typed "beautiful woman" into yahoo, your web page would be the first result.

92. Being as hot as you are, don't you have a hard time not melting your keyboard?

93. Tell me, who's the real person behind the hot picture?

Chapter 12
Mall Pick-Up Lines

You don't hear many stories of people meeting in the mall but that shouldn't stop you. The mall is a very conductive location for meeting women. Consider a woman's mood when she is in a shopping state of mind. She is doing one of her favorite things in the world: buying clothes!

Use her positive state of mind to your advantage. Go get them!

. Do you know where the coed fitting rooms are?

. (You trying on new pants): What do you think about these pants on me? Do I look hot or sexy?

  • Always set yourself up with positives.

. (You trying on new pants): Do you think these pants are tight enough?

  • Getting her to look at your butt is a good start. Shake your ass for extra laughs.

. It's a long line, do you want to share a fitting room?

. Did you just come out of the beauty salon or do you always look that good?

. Will you be my sugar mama and take me shopping for the day?

. What are you shopping for when you already look so fine?

  • Can lead to a provocative conversation about a woman's compulsion to shop.

. The mall should pay you for walking around here, looking so fine. You're like the main attraction.

9. I bet you witness a lot of girlfriends slapping their boyfriends when you walk by huh?

10. A lady of your beauty should not have to walk in here, hop on my shoulders

11. Excuse me, do you know where I can get one of you around here?

12. Shouldn't you be walking down a runway or something?

13. Excuse me, I'm doing a survey on phone numbers. What's yours?

    • For those in the don't know: Survey companies are often found in mall soliciting opinions.

14. Excuse me, I'm giving out a free trial today.

    • If she asks "A free trial of what?" you can respond with: "A free trial of ME!"

    • For those in the don't know: Food stores in malls commonly give out free samples.

15. Excuse me, my store is giving out free kisses today.

16. What time is your dad picking you up?

    • For maximum comedic effect use this on an older woman (twenty-five or older).

17. Excuse me, do you know if they have a designated area in the mall for making out?

18. Do you know what's better than shopping? ME!

19. When you're done shopping I could use some dinner.

    • Build your ego and they will come.

20. Why is it that women love to shop and men could care less?

    • This line can lead to a provocative conversation about man vs. woman shopping behavior.

21. (You trying on new pants): How do these pants make my butt look?

22. (You trying on a new shirt): Does this shirt make you want me?

23. (To a dressing room clerk): It would be a lot easier if you would come in my dressing room and help me out.

24. The only thing I want in this store is you.

25. (To a store clerk): Can you help me find your phone number?

26. (To a store clerk): Will you love me if I buy a lot of things from you?

27. (To a store clerk): Are your mannequins for sale?

    • Make sure that you have your smile on when you deliver this line so you don't look like some perverted freak.

28. Do you know where the love store is?

    • You can follow this with: "You know, the store where you and I fall in love."

29. I didn't see you come in.

    • For maximum comedic effect, ask this to a girl in the middle of the mall.

30. Malls make me mad because I have to get out of my car and walk around.

31. Do you know where I can get any sugar around here?

    • For those in the don't know: Sugar is synonymous with love and affection.

32. Did you know that there is an error in the bible? Where it says "and on the seventh day God rested" what really happened was that God went to the mall.

33. Did you know that there is an error in the bible? Where it says "and on the seventh day God rested" what really happened was that on the seventh day God created the shopping mall.

34. I'm not sure what to price myself, what do you think?

35. Twenty-four-hour-a-day businesses are everywhere. Why isn't there a twenty-four-hour mall?

36. I'm thinking about starting a franchise called 24 Hour Mall, kind of like 24 Hour Fitness. What do you think?

37. Do you think I need an Extreme Makeover?

    • For those in the don't know: "Extreme Makeover" is a reality show where an average Joe/Jane gets numerous cosmetic surgeries.

38. How would you rate my dress: debonair, chic, or stunning?

    • Always put yourself in a positive light.

39. Do you know if there's a Santa Clause in the mall? I was thinking about getting a picture.

    • This works best if it's not the Christmas season. She'll love your sense of humor.

40. Do you know if there's a Santa Clause in the mall? I need a few things that I can't afford, like a hot girlfriend.

41. Is it weird that I occasionally check out mannequins?

    • It's common knowledge that every year the mannequins in department stores are made hotter and hotter.

42. If you happen to be shopping for a man, I'll be around for another hour or so.

43. If you happen to be shopping for a man, they have a great one down at the ME store.

44. If you're returning a boyfriend today, I know a great one down at the ME store.

45. I don't have a price tag on me, because I'm priceless.

46. I can't find your price tag. Are you priceless?

47. Would you hold it against me if I have a no return policy?

48. My return policy is that if you don't like it, you get the next one free.

   • This line is best used on a woman that looks a bit wild because ninety-nine percent of the time "it" will be interpreted as "sex."

49. Some girls treat me like a dress from a department store. They use me and then return me.

50. If you steal me, I won't tell anyone.

51. I don't take cash or cards, just phone numbers.

52. Can you be bought?

   • This line can lead to a provocative conversation about prostitution.

53. If you were a product you would be in a store called Heaven.

54. Are you the latest model of Beautiful?

55. Are you giving out free samples today?

56. Are you giving out kiss samples today?

57. Are you lost, can't find your mommy?

58. Are you lost, cause I'll be your daddy?

59. Excuse me, do you know where I can get a date around here?

60. Excuse me, can you tell me where I can find your phone number around here?

61. I'm thinking about opening my own store in the mall called You Are Fine. What do you think?

62. If I owned a store here you could shoplift from me anytime you wanted.

63. Can you tell me what Victoria's Secret is because I have no idea?

64. You women have Victoria's Secret, how come us guys don't have a Victor's Secret?

65. They have a store called Seventeen, why not a store called Twenty-Three (or whatever your age is)?

66. The only Hot Topic that I can find around here is you.

   • For those in the don't know: Hot Topic is a mall store catering to the youth that sells gothic and novelty items.

67. I'm thinking about opening a store called Devon Wild (insert your name). What do you think?

68. I got my parking validated but I was wondering if you could validate my ego with your phone number?

69. Excuse me, do you validate kisses?

70. Excuse me, but can you validate my attraction to you?

71. What time do YOU close?

72. Have you ever thought about opening a store called The Most Prettiest Girl In The World? You could even abbreviate it TMPGITW.

73. Excuse me ma'am, I think you dropped my phone number.

   • This works best if you have some sort of business card to hand the lady.

74. Is there room in your shopping bag for me?

75. Are you returnable?

76. You know what would look great on you? ME!

77. I want to let you in on a little secret. The Banana Republic sells clothes not fruit.

78. You might want to go to Big 5 and get some kneepads because with the number of bags you have, you might actually "shop till you drop."

79. Women have shopping, men have Playboy, what's the big deal?

80. Do you know where I can get a spanking around here?

1. I don't see your price tag. Are you for sale?

2. (To a girl in a store): What are your washing instructions?

3. How come they don't have carts at the mall like they do at the grocery store?

   • She'll be intrigued by your acute observation of shopping environments.

4. Why do they call it "window shopping" when no one actually buys windows?

5. How are you supposed to make me dinner when you're buying clothes instead of groceries?

6. I bet if they had a frequent maller program you would have already won your own mall by now.

7. I bet that I would look great on you.

8. I bet you would look great on me.

9. If I like to shop does that mean I'm gay?

0. I don't see a tag on me, so I guess that means you can have me for free.

1. What do you think about America's dependency on credit cards and consumerism?

   • This is best used on a nerdy-looking hot girl.

2. Excuse me, I'm looking for something that can hold me and love me. Do you know if they have anything like that around here?

Chapter 13
Rude And Crude Pick-Up Lines

Rude And Crude Pick-Up Lines are to be used when you're looking for a one-night stand. There is no going back once you unleash one of these lascivious lines.

Watch out for the slaps and drinks but used upon the right girl you'll be appreciated for your gutsy advance. These lines are best used for girls that are smoking (studies show that women who smoke cigarettes are more promiscuous), wearing revealing clothing, or parading around drunk and obnoxious.

Feel free to use Rude And Crude Pick-Up Lines upon a woman of a more pristine nature but beware of the consequences. Good luck! Go get them!

1. Just in case it crossed your mind, I'm not wearing any underwear.

2. Let's dump society's laws and regulations and do it right here on the bar.

3. I know what you're thinking. Will this guy be able to get his whisky dick up when I ravage him. That's why I brought my Viagra.

4. I'll show you mine if you show me yours.

5. I just want to let you know that those penis pumps work.

6. (To a girl smoking a cigarette): Are you practicing?

    • If she seems dumbfounded by this line you can follow with: "You know, for later tonight."

7. Wouldn't it be cool if we just turned this place into an orgy bar? Just drunk copious sex.

8. I'm not charging tonight. This one's on me.

   • If she says "charging for what" you can say: "My sexual healing."

9. You look just like this girl in the porno I was watching last night.

10. If you're looking for a night of debauchery then I'm your man.

11. Would you hold it against me if I told you I was hung like a T-Rex?

   • T-Rex is short for Tyrannosaurus Rex, one of the largest dinosaurs to have ever lived.

12. I think I saw you on an episode of "Cops" in New Orleans flashing your boobs for beads. Was that you?

13. How much is it going to take for us to hit the sheets tonight?

   • To get the maximum comedic value out of this line it's important to take out your wallet as you're saying it. You can even take the comedic value further by pulling out one-dollar bills out of your wallet.

14. Would you hold it against me if I told you that I regularly take girls out of here and go to the Motel 6?

15. Would you hold it against me if I told you I had a twelve-inch cock?

16. (To a girl sucking on a straw from a mixed drink): I'm jealous of your straw.

17. I wish I was your underwear.

18. I may be dull, poor, and ugly, but I'm hung like a horse.

19. Some guys work out their bodies, I work out my tongue.

20. How many people in the world do you think are orgasming right this very second?

   • You can follow this with: "How come orgasms only last a few seconds?"

21. Your aura tells me that you have sex often. Is this true?

22. Why do they call it "doggie-style" when lion, tigers, and bears do it that way too? How come they don't call it "lion-style?"

23. "Blowjob" seems like a misnomer. Shouldn't they be called "suckjobs?"

24. (Point to your sides): Some call these "love handles" but I prefer to call them "blowjob handles."

25. You seem like a respectable young lady, but I bet behind that respectable façade is a little slut. Fuck me if I'm wrong, but am I right?

26. I couldn't help but notice that you were sizing up my manhood.

    • It doesn't matter whether she was or wasn't, just tell her.

27. Does size really matter?

    • The classic question still reigns supreme.

28. Would you hold it against me if I told you I was hung like a mouse?

29. (To two girls talking): Are you girls talking about hot dogs?

    • If they reply "no" a great follow up is: "Damn!"

30. (To a girl smoking a cigarette): Do you really like to smoke cigarettes or are you trying to tell me something?

31. Is today free pink taco Saturday (insert the proper day of the week)?

    • For those in the don't know: "Pink taco" is a sexual innuendo for "pussy."

32. I like your Halloween costume.

    • This is best used on a hot chick that is suffering from too many compliments. Sometimes using a derogatory remark will get you positive attention.

33. When I play doctor I prefer to be a gynecologist. What about yourself?

34. Are those thimbles on your chest, or are you happy to see me?

    • A comedic female spin on the classic pick-up line: "Is that a banana in your pants or are you happy to see me?"

35. Why do you have all those clothes on for?

    • To get maximum comedic value out of this line it's best used on a woman who isn't wearing much clothing.

36. Let's go skinny-dipping and pretend my bed is the lake! What do you say?

37. I'm offering free massages at my private practice. Boob massages that is. Would you like to set up an appointment?

38. Would you like a free boob massage, they're the newest rage?

39. You look like you could use a real spank on the ass. When was your last spanking?

40. What's all this sixty-nine business, I don't get it?

    • For those in the don't know: The term "sixty-nine" is commonly known as the oral sex position that enables both man and woman to give and receive oral pleasure at the same time. Examine the number carefully and it will all make sense. 69.

41. My fortune cookie said my lucky number was sixty-nine. Does that number have any significance?

42. It's my birthday, and I'm giving you the honor of spanking me.

    • It doesn't matter whether it's your birthday or not.

43. Is it your birthday, because I would love to spank you?

44. Didn't I make out with you at that party last year?

    • You can follow this up with: "I remember you being an awesome groper."

45. You look delicious.

46. I just want to let you know that I have no quirps about sex in public: bar, car, park, it's all good.

47. (Singing like Enrique Iglesias in his "Hero" song): I will be your popsicle baby.

48. I hear you give good conversation.

    - For those in the don't know: This line is a comedic spin on the oral sex phrase "give good head."

49. I'm doing free ass readings tonight. When you're ready just pull down your pants.

50. There are no height limitations for this ride.

51. I bet you're a vegetarian. You like to eat things like cucumbers and carrots huh?

52. I'll bark like a dog, meow like a cat, whatever you want.

53. I noticed that you use a straw with your drink. Why is that?

54. Would you hold it against me if I told you that you could make a lot of money in porn?

55. Don't forget your underwear tomorrow morning.

    - She'll love your presumptuousness.

56. (To a woman holding a bottle of beer): How do you like holding that beer (bottle)?

    - Some say that a beer bottle is symbolic of a man's penis.

57. Do you ever drink two beers at the same time?

58. I can hold my breath for sixty-nine seconds. What about you?

59. I have stamina and I'm not talking about running marathons.

60. You have a beautiful mouth.

61. In what ways would you find yourself similar to a vacuum cleaner?

62. Sigmond Freud said that if you dream of trees that you are dreaming about penises and that if you dream of tunnels that you are dreaming about vaginas. Do you think that's true?

53. Have you ever noticed that everything is phallic? You know, the Freudian term for genitalia shaped objects: beers, door knobs, lipstick, the Space Needle in Seattle. What do you think of that?

54. Do you know what the lyrics are for the chorus of the Nine Inch Nails song "Closer?"

   • For those in the don't know: The lyrics are: "I want to fuck you like an animal, I want to feel you from the inside."

     Note: If you ever want to incorporate other lyrics into this pick-up line, a great resource is www.sing365.com which has the lyrics for just about every popular song ever written.

55. Can you touch your toes?

   • No matter whether she tells you "yes" or "no" tell her to "prove it." That is if you want to see her bend over and show you that nice ass. This is better used on the younger women because the older women have caught on to such juvenile tricks.

56. Can you touch your elbows together behind your back?

   • No matter whether she tells you "yes" or "no" tell her to "prove it." That is if you want to see her push her boobs out. This is better used on the younger women because the older women have caught on to such juvenile tricks.

57. Don't make me get oral.

58. Wouldn't it be cool if you could maintain that feeling of orgasm 24-7-365?

59. Are you thinking what I'm thinking?

   • If she says "what are you thinking" you should reply with one of the following:

     • "Skinny dipping!"

     • "Hot sex!"

     • "The number sixty-nine!"

60. I saw the movie "Fight Club" and I got inspired so I started Fuck Club. Want to join?

71. Can you fit your fist in your mouth?

   • If she attempts this dare then you found your girl.

72. I'll buy you a beer but consider that beer your breakfast for tomorrow morning.

73. I'll buy you a beer if you can guess the size of my swartz.

74. What can a dollar get me?

   • A funny follow up for this pick-up line is: "How about a quarter?"

75. What do you like better: shopping or orgasms?

76. I have to get up for work in the morning so you can't spend the night.

   • Always assume that she wants you.

77. I am sex incarnate.

   • For those in the don't know: *Webster's Encyclopedic Unabridged Dictionary* defines incarnate as "1. Embodied in flesh; given a bodily, esp. a human form. 2. Personified or typified, as a quality or idea."

78. (To a girl with a friend): Is it two for one night?

79. I'm not looking at your boobs; I'm staring at them.

80. You're such a tease with that bottle of beer.

81. Would you describe yourself as easy or hard?

82. What do you like better: watching a good romantic comedy or cunnilingus?

83. What do you think of pogo sticks?

   • For those in the don't know: *Random House Webster's College Dictionary* defines pogo stick as "a long stick with footrests and a spring, used as a toy for leaping." It could be associated with the up and down motion of sex.

84. Do you have a free trial period?

85. Do you take quarters?

86. Have you ever met a man that was bent?

   - For those in the don't know: Bent's common definition is "corrupt" but a small percentage of men have a unit that when erect is "bent" like a boomerang. Let the girl take it where she wants to take it.

87. Are you taking the twins for a night out?

   - The "twins" is a sexual innuendo for "tits."

88. If the twins need babysitting, I'll take care of them.

89. Is it your birthday because you look like you could use a spanking?

90. Are you the door prize tonight?

91. Do you cum often?

92. I've been bad. Will you spank me?

93. I was wondering if you're busy next Friday at 2:00 in the morning?

94. Do you receive a lot of packages?

   - For those in the don't know: "Package" is a sexual innuendo for "penis."

95. Your voice sounds familiar. Do you work in the nine-seven-six business?

96. So who do you like to do?

   - This is a sexual twist on the common but boring icebreaker question: "So what do you do?"

97. Is money out of the question?

98. Did you know the street you live on and your pet's name combined is your porn star name?

99. If you are looking for a revenge-fuck to get back at your boyfriend, I'm your man.

100. Is it true that girls size up guys' packages?

- Best used in a party atmosphere. Also better if used on a group of two or more girls so as not to make one girl feel awkward. Can lead to a funny conversation about the secret ways of women.

101. I'm tiny (followed with a hand signature that your unit is small).

- Women, especially the naïve and young, are so thrown off by something this brazen and strange that it positively intrigues them. The girls will also appreciate your self-effacing humor.

Chapter 14
Party Pick-Up Lines

A party is the perfect place to unleash pick-up lines because the ladies are ready for a wild and crazy time. Women go to parties to have a great time but they're always hoping that they're going to meet some amazing guy. That amazing guy is YOU! Go get them!

1. Is this your birthday party because I'm a professional spanker?

2. This guy down the hall told me you're his girlfriend and it's OK if we make out.

   • If you don't want to get your ass kicked you had better find out if she came with a boyfriend before you dish out this pick-up line.

3. I heard you're a good kisser. Is this true?

4. When you're ready to make out, I'll be right here.

5. I'll trade sex for drugs if you got any. Or sex for sex.

6. You're a hot drunk.

7. Are the drugs getting to me or are you amazingly hot?

8. I'm a sensitive guy. If you start puking your brains out I'll take care of you.

   • She'll love your tender vulgarity.

9. That's funny, because I didn't hear the hot detector go off when you came in.

10. You're hot, I'm hot, let's get it on.

11. Don't you think it would be really weird if we didn't make out tonight?

12. Can I ask you a serious question? What are the chances of us making out tonight?

13. I'm doing auditions for my new movie called "Making Out." What time do you want to audition?

14. Something smells wonderful. Is that your perfume or the keg?

15. Tonight's your night. I'll do whatever you want: slap you, kiss you, whip you, lick you, whatever. What's it going to be?

16. Do you offer an extra value meal?

17. How hard do you party?

18. What's your major, Party Sciences?

19. Who do you think is the hottest guy here besides me?

20. This is a private party, let's see your privates.

21. I don't take reservations, it's first come first serve.

22. The first step in (your name) Anonymous, is to overcome your denial.

    • This is a comedic spin on the twelve-step alcohol recovery program Alcoholics Anonymous.

23. I'm not harmful if swallowed.

24. I'm highly addictive so just be prewarned.

25. This isn't a Halloween party.

    • If she seems dumbfounded you can follow with: "Well you're dressed up as a supermodel aren't you?"

26. Why don't you pretend that I'm Santa Clause. Sit on my lap and tell me what you want.

27. I have some lust if you want some.

28. You know this is an orgy party, right?

29. You know this is a panty party, right?

30. Are you the stripper I ordered?

31. If you put roofies in my drink and take advantage of me, I have no problems with that.

    • For those in the don't know: "Roofies" is the street name for a date-rape drug that enhances the effects of alcohol: decreased inhibition, sleepiness, and memory loss.

32. I hope you don't mind me saying so but you appear to be extremely horny.

33. Why did God let women have multiple orgasms and only give man his one? Maybe God makes mistakes too.

34. You look so exotic. Do you have a website or something?

35. No, I won't sign your boobs.

    • Your presumptuousness will bring a smile to her face.

36. Yes, I'm for real.

    • A good follow up is: "Go ahead and pinch yourself, you're not dreaming."

37. If I can feel yours, you can feel mine.

38. My personality isn't my strong point. It's my love making skills.

39. Can I ask you a personal question? Do you get drunk and do things that you often regret because if you're like that, that's exactly what I'm looking for?

40. Psychology says the more you're exposed to something, the more you'll like it. So you can count on seeing me many times tonight.

    • This has been confirmed by many scientific studies.

41. My mom told me never to talk to strangers, but how am I ever supposed to meet anyone?

    • Sometimes acting like a child wins smiles. Just ask Adam Sandler.

42. If the band doesn't show up, would you mind stripping or singing accapela No Doubt?

43. Are you the girl in that "Girls Gone Wild" video?

44. Do you have your boyfriend resume on you? I want to see what I'm dealing with here.

45. Show me that you're not completely crazy and give me a generous French kiss.

    • Sometimes it's necessary to con a woman into a kiss.

46. If two plus two equals four how come ten keeps popping into my mind?

    • For those in the don't know: The "ten" mentioned above is in reference to man's rating system for women in which a "perfect ten" is the top score a woman can receive.

47. The type of job I had in mind for you has nothing to do with resumes.

48. I heard the world is going to end tonight. Let's go out with a bang?

49. I'm going to make this incredibly clear to you. I'm a sure thing.

50. You have to be at least five feet to ride this ride.

51. I know you've had boyfriends before but have you ever had a MAN FRIEND?

52. The clothes aren't really necessary.

53. I heard you're wanted in fifty states, but I'm not talking about the law.

54. What did you bring for Show And Tell?

55. I'm into business. The orgasm business. Would you like a free sample?

56. Call your dad and tell him that I'll have you back by lunch tomorrow.

57. Call your boyfriend and tell him you just met a MANFRIEND.

58. I promise I'll make you a great breakfast tomorrow morning.

    • Assume that the deal will be sealed and your confidence will win her over.

59. I've watched "E.R." for a number of years so if you need a physical just let me know.

60. You weren't that girl I had a one-night stand with last year are you?

61. Would you object to a wet T-shirt contest without the contest?

62. Are you here for your make out appointment?

63. Did you think you were going skiing tonight? You don't need all those clothes.

    • This line works for maximum comedic value if the girl isn't wearing much to begin with.

64. What do you want to name our kids?

    • You can follow this up with: "I like those long names like 'MommyAnd-DaddyMetAtAParty.'"

65. Would you consider yourself slutty?

    • You can follow this with: "That's what I look for in a woman."

66. I'm all bark and no bite but I'll bite if you want me to.

67. If you can't afford me I have a monthly plan.

    • It's never too late to get into male prostitution.

68. How am I suppose to really know you with all of those clothes on?

69. I'm shooting a new video called "Hot Girls Show Their Boobies." Do you want to participate?

70. What was the name of that Color Me Bad song? "I Want To Sex You Up" or something?

    • This is an indirect way of telling a girl that you want to get in her pants.

71. I have a money back guarantee. If after thirty days you don't like me I'll refund all the gifts that you bought me.

72. Ah, we both have something in common I see. We both like G-STRINGS.

    • This pick-up line is to be used on a girl that is obviously wearing a G-string.

73. I worship the God Dionysus. He is the Roman god of fertility and wine.

74. Why can't you come in my cereal box?

75. Can I get you a something: beer, Everclear, a kiss?

76. I believe in giving. Please take my virginity or lack there of.

77. Are you one of the Bud Light Girls?

78. So what are your features and benefits?

    • She'll laugh when you treat her like a product.

79. Are you the entertainment?

80. I thought I was the most beautiful, but maybe I am mistaken.

81. If this was a Halloween party I would guess that you're dressed up as The Most Beautiful Girl That Ever Lived.

82. Excuse me, I didn't mean to take your breadth away. Do you need mouth-to-mouth resuscitation?

83. What kind of drunk are you?

    • This line can lead to a provocative conversation about the variety of drunks: bitter, happy, mad, sad, etc.

84. I bet even when you puke you still look good.

    • Nothing like using vulgarity to pay a compliment.

85. What do you think I'm wearing: boxers, briefs, or bare pickle?

86. I guess instead of a catered dessert they just brought you instead.

87. I'm not a lawyer or a doctor, but I like to watch them on television. Are you still impressed?

88. If we don't hit it off do you have a twin sister?

89. Have you ever fallen in love with your own reflection like the ancient Greek myth of Narcissus?

    • For those in the don't know: According to *Webster's Encyclopedic Unabridged Dictionary* "Narcissus was a mythic youth who fell in love with his own image reflected in a pool and wasted away from unsatisfied desire, whereupon he was transformed into the flower known today as narcissus."

    • Can lead to a provocative conversation about narcissism.

90. As a man I love you but if I were a woman I would hate you.

91. Wait a minute, is this a party or a beauty pageant?

92. Tell me how it feels to be desired by every man and woman alive?

93. Nice to meet you, I'm…..speechless.

    • Extend your hand out for a handshake when you deliver this line.

94. Nice to meet you, I'm……enamored.

    • Extend your hand out for a handshake when you deliver this line.

95. Nice to meet you, I'm…..sprung.

    • Extend your hand out for a handshake when you deliver this line.

96. Nice to meet you, I'm…..dumbfounded.

    • Extend your hand out for a handshake when you deliver this line.

97. Nice to meet you, I'm…..enthralled.

    • Extend your hand out for a handshake when you deliver this line.

Chapter 15
Video Store Pick-Up Lines

The video store is a very neglected location for meeting women. Don't be like the other soft guys in the store who are going home wishing they had a girl to watch the movie with. Utilize Video Store Pick-Up Lines and take the video and the girl home. Go get them!

1. Have you seen that movie where the girl falls for the guy at the video store?

    • You can follow this up with: "I think it stars you and me."

2. (To girls checking out horror movies): Hey if you girls need a guy to hold onto when you're watching your horror movie, I'm available tonight.

3. Was that movie "The Hot Chick" about you?

4. Do you know if they have porno movies here?

5. Was that "Star Wars" movie based on a true story?

6. You're so fine, you should be making movies not watching movies.

7. Some call me old-fashioned but I still like watching movies on VHS.

8. If you were a movie it would be called "The Hottest Girl That Ever Lived."

9. If you were a movie it would be called "Supermodel."

10. If you were a movie, it would be called "Special."

11. If you were a movie, it would be called "Distraction."

12. I would rather watch you than a movie.

13. Hey, if you're going to get a romance, skip the movie and have me over instead.

14. Why pay for entertainment when you can have me for free?

15. What the hell is a DVD player?

   • Sometimes it's fun to play dumb just to let her feel smart.

16. For $1.99 you could have popcorn with that movie or you could have me. What's it going to be?

17. I hope I don't sound cheap but for the price of that movie rental you could have me for a week.

18. Are you old enough to be watching rated R movies?

   • For maximum comedic effect use this line on an older woman (twenty-five or older) who obviously is old enough to rent rated R movies.

19. Did you really come here to rent a movie or to meet eligible bachelors?

20. Are you having a pajama party tonight because I can run home and get mine?

21. How about you get the movie and I'll bring the beer?

22. I have a bad back, can you reach down and grab that movie for me?

   • Not so much of a pick-up line as much as it is just a chance for you to see a hot girl bend over and show you her nice ass.

23. I'm not due back the next day.

24. If your VCR/DVD is broken you can watch that movie over at my place.

25. I bet that they could make a movie based on your beauty.

26. I bet that they could make a movie based on your smile.

27. Do you rewind your DVDs before you bring them back?

   • You'll be surprised how many girls will laugh at stupid humor.

28. (To a girl looking at a movie box): You know I was going to get that movie too. What do you say we split the price and watch it at my place?

29. I have a free tip for you: sit real close to your television and then you'll feel like you're at the movie theater.

30. Taking a night off from all those nasty men?

31. Do you know what's a lot more enjoyable than a movie? ME!

32. Don't you think they should have a money back guarantee for movies? You can return almost anything else. If a movie sucks it should say so on the box.

    • She'll admire your astute observation of the unfair nature of the movie marketplace.

33. If they made a movie based on your life story what would it be called?

34. If they made a movie about me it would be called "The Guy That Fell In Love With The Girl At The Video Store."

35. I can totally see you on a video box.

36. What time is your mom picking you up?

    • This is best used on an older woman for maximum comedic affect.

37. If you're going to rent one of those superhero movies you might as well just rent me.

38. What time do I have to return you by?

39. What's your story?

40. How does the story of you and I go?

41. How does the story of you and I end?

42. Is this where our story begins?

43. What happens after hello?

44. How come there aren't more scenes in movies that take place in the video store?

45. Do you have any sequels?

    • When she looks dumbfounded you can say: "You know, any little brothers or sisters?"

46. Would you ever date one of those hot older guys like George Clooney or Clint Eastwood?

47. (Strike a pose): Do you think I have star power?

48. Do you think Freddy Kreuger is gay because I never see him hooking up with any chicks?

    • For those in the don't know: Freddy Kreuger is the haunting demon in the "Nightmare On Elm Street" horror movie series.

49. Do you think movie stars are really as cool as they think they are?

    • This line can lead to a riveting conversation about narcissism.

50. You know there are two kinds of people in life: people who watch movies and people who live like movies. Screw the movie rental, let's fall in love tonight and take over the world. What do you think?

51. Why is it so important to find Nemo?

52. Why would you want to see/rent "Master and Commander" when you can have one?

53. You know I'm thinking about filming a short movie called "What's Your Phone Number" starring you and me. What do you think?

54. How interested would you be in a movie called "Flirting At The Video Store" starring you and me?

55. (At Blockbuster Video): I saw Tom Cruise has a parking spot outside. Do you see him in here much?

   • For those in the don't know: Blockbuster Video has movie star names printed on the parking spaces at all of their stores to make it seem more like a magical experience renting movies.

56. Do you think stars watch their own movies a lot?

57. If you really want to see drama you should come over to my house/apartment and see my goldfish/parents/Sea Monkies/roommates go at it.

58. What do you think my movie title would be if I had a movie besides "Mr. Perfect" of course?

59. Is "Pulp Fiction" based on a true story?

60. I hate the three-night rental because by the fourth day you forget you even rented the damn movie.

   • This line can lead to a provocative conversation about the conspiracy of Blockbuster Video to loot the American public of their hard-earned money through late fees.

61. I have this idea for a movie: "Three Girls Fighting Over Me." What do you think?

62. I see you've been in here for awhile. Are you sure you don't want me for your entertainment tonight?

63. What do you think about guys that sneak food into the theater: bad boy, thrifty, or embarrassing cheapskate?

64. I'm only a dollar and you can keep me for six nights.

65. I thought "XXX" was a porno film, but when I got home and put it in the VCR I found out it's a retarded movie about a dumb bald guy running around spitting out stupid lines. Did the same thing happen to you?

66. How come Jaws hasn't gotten any roles lately? You think they would have given him a cameo in "Free Willy."

67. Does that FBI copyright warning at the beginning of the tape scare you a little bit even though you haven't done anything wrong?

68. Keep in mind when you're looking that I don't have any late fees.

69. (To a girl at Blockbuster Video): Don't you think it's kind of a sham that this place is called Blockbuster Video when most of the movies weren't blockbusters?

70. "Free Willy" sounds like a dirty movie to me.

    • For those in the don't know: "Willy" is a sexual innuendo for "penis."

71. How come the good guys always win in movies?

    • This line can lead to a provocative conversation about the formulaic ways of Hollywood.

72. Would you date a guy here just so you could get free movie rentals?

73. You know I rented "Animal House" the other night and I don't think their was one animal in the whole movie. What's up with that?

    • This is best used on older women (twenty-five or older) who have seen this classic comedy of yesterday.

74. If you decide to rent a horror movie and you need a guy to hold on to during the scary scenes, I'm available tonight.

75. You know I watched that "Scary Movie" the other night and that wasn't a scary movie.

    • She'll love your sarcasm.

76. So, how long have you been watching movies?

77. If you like long passionate love scenes you don't need a movie. You need ME!

78. I heard every movie in here sucks. Why don't we get coffee instead.

79. "When Harry Met Sally" was a great movie but "When I Met You" sounds even better.

80. What are you rated? G, PG, PG-13, R, NC-17, X, or XXX?

   - You might want to leave off the X and XXX so she doesn't think that you're some porno freak. That is unless she looks like a porno freak herself.

81. How come Blockbuster doesn't have any XXX movies? Isn't that discriminatory?

82. I'm R rated but just for nudity.

83. I'm G during the day but NC-17 at night.

84. You look PG-13 but I bet after you loosen up you're at least R and possibly NC-17.

85. If you were a movie, what genre would you be? Drama, comedy, horror, action, suspense-thriller, or porno?

   - You might want to leave off porno if she doesn't look like a porn star.

86. (To a girl reading a movie box): You can read?

   - She'll appreciate your sarcasm.

87. Can I ask you a serious question? Do you prefer Red Vines or Twizzlers?

88. Does your mom know what kind of movies you're looking at?

89. (To a girl at Blockbuster Video): Do you think the stars have to pay for their parking spots outside?

90. I'm going to let you in on a little secret. If you don't want anybody sitting in front of you or next to you at the movie theater just dump some pop on the seats.

91. If Julia Roberts and Tom Cruise didn't have great smiles do you think they would still be movie stars?

   - This line can lead to a riveting conversation about the power of smiles on the psyche.

92. Don't you think The Rock was kind of being modest with his name? He should have named himself Boulder or Big Rock at least.

93. You have a movie star smile.

94. Who do you think the worst/best actor/actress in Hollywood is?

95. A UCLA film professor once said that all screenplays are based on personal, life experiences of the screenwriter. So do you think Freddy Krueger (or whomever you want) was based on a real person?

96. (In your Old-Man-Trailer/Preview Voice): Once upon a time there was a beautiful girl, who fell for a boy, in a video store..... (fill in the rest with your unique situation).

97. Do you know if they have "Pinocchio Uncut?"

    • Some say that Pinocchio's nose resembles a penis.

98. (To a girl at Blockbuster Video): How come they don't have a parking spot for Hannibal Lector outside?

99. Do you think it's true that people go to the movies/ because their own lives suck?/ because their own lives are a dreary bore?

Chapter 16
Walking Pick-Up Lines

Picking up women while walking is another great opportunity that many bachelors never take advantage of. This is one of those situations in which you'll most likely never see the girl again so you have absolutely nothing to lose.

If you are walking the same direction as the hottie you'll have plenty of time to roll out PJCSP. However, if she's coming from the opposite direction then make sure that your smile is shining and then deliver one your favorite Walking Pick-Up Lines from your mental arsenal. If she stops, then proceed through the full PJCSP assault. If she's in a hurry but seems responsive go straight from P to P. That is from pick-up line to phone number.

Remember you have nothing to lose. Go get them!

1. Were you at that party last week?

    - Make up some party that you didn't go to. People who go to parties are seen as fun and likeable people for the most part. Once you start dating she'll forgive you for the little white lie that you told her to get her attention.

2. You're walking! I'm walking! What are the chances?

3. Slow down there speedy. You're going to hit somebody.

4. I like your gait.

    - For those in the don't know: gait is the manner of one's walking, stepping, or running.

5. Isn't walking underrated?

    • The line can lead to a provocative conversation about how the proliferation of the automobile has played a major role in the burgeoning obesity of America.

6. You know what I like about walking? You don't have to have any insurance.

7. It's a nice day for falling in love isn't it?

8. Quit swerving.

    • You can follow this with: "Are you drunk walking?"
    • You can use this regardless of whether she's swerving.

9. Excuse me, have you been drinking and walking ma'am?

10. When was the last time you got a tune-up?

11. Want to race?

12. You're in the wrong lane.

    • Depending on how fast she's walking you can point out the proper lane on the sidewalk.

13. Do you have a walking license?

14. Do you have insurance for those legs?

    • For those in the don't know: *The Sun* and the *New York Post* ran articles in 1999 claiming that J-Lo had insured her body for 1 billion dollars. The report claimed that her breasts were appraised at 100 million each and her legs and ass combined were valued at 300 million.

15. You're lucky they don't inforce insurance for walking because your leg insurance would be in the millions.

16. Can I get a ride?

    • You can follow this with: "I prefer to be in your arms but piggyback is fine too."

17. Do you mind if I piggyback?

18. You know the walking speed is only two mph around here so you better watch it.

19. What walking school did you graduate from?

20. What year did you finish walking school?

21. Did you get your masters in walking because your gait is extraordinary?

22. Did you start walking earlier than other toddlers because your gait is amazing?

23. Have you ran into any traffic today?

    • You can follow this with: "You know: old ladies, drunk walkers, dog poop."

24. You're not sleep walking are you? I just don't want you to get hurt.

25. How's your walking record?

    • You can follow this with: "Has your beauty been the catalyst for many accidents?"

26. How are your brakes?

    • If she seems receptive give her a little push so she can test her human breaks. Just don't push her very hard. Flirt don't hurt.

27. Do you ever make the transition to the Speed Walk?

    • For those in the don't know: The Speed Walk was a ridiculous walk/run hybrid that had a short-lived existence in the 1980s. The short-lived existence was due mainly to the fact that people looked like complete idiots when they were doing it.

28. Do you drink and walk?

29. Been in many accidents?

30. Do you have a good walking history?

31. Do you have anything against the bicycle?

32. I'm giving rides for a dollar.

    • You can follow this with: "One dollar per pound that is."

33. How many miles do you have on those shoes?

34. Are you at top speed right now?

    • For those in the don't know: America's Maurice Greene is the fastest recorded running human being who reached a top speed of twenty-seven mph in Athens Greece on June 16, 1999.

35. If you could patent your walk you would be very rich.

36. Are you taking your sweet ass for a walk?

    • Watch out for the slaps from the pristine girls.

37. I'm taking my ass for a walk, what about yourself?

38. What do you think about those automobiles?

    • She'll love your sarcasm.

39. Are you training for a walk-a-thon or something?

40. What do you think of those treadmills?

41. What are you in a hurry for? I'm right here.

42. Is that ass street legal?

43. What exit are you taking?

44. Are you on cruise control?

45. I bet you would be able to walk faster if you unloaded your phone number.

46. If I had a horn I would honk.

    • You can follow this with: "You're walking a little to slow to be in the fast lane."

47. What's your zero to five mph time?

48. Have you ever had a walking accident?

49. What do you think of Speed Walking?

50. When was the last time that you got a tune-up?

    • If she looks dumbfounded you can follow with: "You know, a knee massage or change of shoes?"

51. Did you eat your Wheaties this morning because you're walking like a champion?

    • For those in the don't know: Wheaties marketing slogan is "The Breakfast of Champions."

52. What's your top speed?

53. A lot of dogs walk this path, so be careful.

54. If it's ever raining you're welcome to walk around in my apartment/house.

55. How's your steering?

56. Nike said "Just Do It" and I guess you did.

    • She'll see the humor in this line regardless of whether she's wearing Nikes.

57. When you pass someone on the left do you say "on your left" or do you just surprise them?

    • This line can lead to a provocative conversation about proper walking etiquette.

58. Do you ever run out of gas?

59. That's a nice ride you got there.

60. How's the sidewalk today?

61. Are these good walking conditions?

52. How's your suspension?

   • If she seems receptive push down on her shoulders lightly as if you're checking the suspension on a car.

53. Are you the Ultimate Walking Machine?

   • For those in the don't know: This is a comedic riff off of BMW's marketing slogan "The Ultimate Driving Machine."

54. Who's in the lead?

55. Want a push?

56. Need a lift?

   • For maximum comedic effect point to your shoulders when you deliver this line.

57. Who's your favorite walker? Jesus? Paul Walker?

   • For those in the don't know: Paul Walker is an actor who's known more for his good looks than his ability to act.

58. Isn't that supposed to be a modeling runway beneath you?

59. Do you know what the speed limit is around here?

70. Do you miss not having all the mirrors that your car has?

71. Do you know if AAA will come and repair my shoes?

72. Do you find it flattering or crass when men honk at you?

73. Does walking run in the family?

   • She'll love your play on words.

74. Which do you prefer: a wider sidewalk or one that is smoothly paved?

75. Jesus was able to walk on water so does that mean he didn't know how to swim?

76. Do you speed up when you get on the freeway?

77. Don't you think they should make more movies about walking?

78. I thought the Miss America Pageant was the opposite direction?

79. Isn't it weird how once we learn how to walk we never crawl anymore?

    • This line can lead to a provocative conversation about bipedal transportation vs. four-legged.

80. Do you think God walks?

    • This line can lead to a riveting conversation about God's transportation or lack there of.

81. You know I heard this walking phenomenon is catching on.

82. That's a lot of beauty to be carrying with you.

83. Do you think you can read someone by the way they walk?

    • This line can lead to a provocative conversation about body language and self expression.

84. How many people in the world do you think are walking right now?

85. Have you ever been in an accident with a drunk walker?

86. Do you think AAA would bring me some water?

87. (On the beach): I forgot my bathing suit, do you have an extra one?

    • The ridiculousness of the question will win you a smile.

88. (On the beach): I heard the best sex is in the water. Is this true?

    • This is best used on women wearing thongs. Beware of the slap.

89. (On the beach): Is this a nude beach?

90. (On the beach): Do you want to start a nude beach?

91. (On the beach): Do you know how to get to the beach from here?

    • Being stupid will often win you laughs and smiles. Just look at the success of Carrot Top.

92. (On the beach): Is your name Sandy?

   • If she doesn't get this line you had better knock on her head to see if it's hollow.

93. (On the beach): Have you seen my whale?

   • This pick-up line can be delivered innocently or sexually. The choice is up to you.

94. (On the beach): Have you tried IT, in the water yet?

   • This pick-up line can be delivered innocently or sexually. The choice is up to you.

95. (On the beach): Have you seen David Hasselhoff around here?

96. (On the beach): I didn't know they are filming Bay Watch today.

Bonus Chapter
The New Spin On "What's Your Sign" Pick-Up Lines

What's your sign? This is perhaps the most famous and the worst pick-up line of all time. Whether or not someone has actually used it successfully has yet to be documented. Remember, the best pick-up lines include three elements: originality, open-ended questioning, and humor. This trite pick-up line has only one of the elements.

In order to use astrology successfully in picking up women you'll need to actually know the characteristics of each sign and apply that knowledge to each specific situation. Astrology is a fascinating field of study that intrigues many women. Study the sign characteristics and the pick-up lines below and you'll see how putting a new spin on "What's your sign?" will win the girls. Go get them!

Pieces
Symbol: Fish
February 19–March 20
Opposite Sign: Virgo

- dance, unusual talent, memory, wisdom, versatility, sensitivity, intuition, humor, satire, secrets, fulfillment of life, eternity, compassion, sympathy, love, altruism, dreams, the psychic, clairvoyance, sixth sense, illusions, magic, film, fantasy, make-believe, art, drama, music, poetry, prose.

1.   You move around like a fish. Are you a Pieces?

2.   You seem to have compassion and sympathy. Are you a Pieces?

3.   Your outfit is like a piece of art. Are you a Pieces?

Aries
Symbol: the Ram
March 21–April 19
Opposite Sign: Libra

- creativity, personal goals, personal control of everything, competition, winning, being first, courage, honesty, nobility, openness, self-assertion, initiation, new beginnings, action, daring, challenge, adventure, aggression.

4.   You move around like a ram. Are you an Aries?

5.   You seem very competitive. Are you an Aries?

Taurus
Symbol: the Bull
April 20–May 20
Opposite Sign: Scorpio

- love of living things, possession, control, security, dependability, habit, organization, tenacity, kindness, shyness, cautiousness, trustworthiness, appreciation, of values, talents, abilities, beauty, romance, sentimentality, sensuality, materialistic values, wealth, prosperity, nature, harmony.

6.   You move around like a bull. Are you a Taurus?

7.   You seem like a gold digger. Are you a Taurus?

8.   You seem in total control. Are you a Taurus?

Gemini
Symbol: the Twins
May 21–June 21
Opposite Sign: Sagittarius

- variety, movement, curiosity, explorations, short journeys, education, learning, collecting facts, attention to details, adaptability, intellect, intuition, youth, freedom, communication, articulation, speech, dexterity, nimbleness, grace, wit, instinct, persuasion, change.

9.   You seem quite articulate and communicative. Are you a Gemini?

10.   You look curious about learning my phone number. Are you a Gemini?

Cancer
ymbol: the Crab
une 21–July 22
Opposite Sign: Capricorn

response to public need, dreams, the psychic, telepathy, family, history, memory, patriotism, receptivity, sensitivity, defense, home, protection, comfort, domesticity, food, nurturing instincts, nostalgia, sentiment, roots, antiques, money, business.

1. I saw you moving like a crab earlier. Are you a Cancer?

2. You have a serenity about you. Are you a Cancer?

Leo
ymbol: the Lion
uly 23–August 22
Opposite Sign: Aquarius

love affairs, sex, offspring, children, childlike activities, childishness, taking risks, gambling, sports, games, performance, drama, limelight, applause, hospitality, appreciation, pleasures, fun, playfulness, entertainment, creativity, recognition, compliments, romance.

3. I saw you moving around like a lion. Are you a Leo?

4. I see you like to show off. Are you a Leo?

5. You seem to be the queen of the bar. Are you a Leo?

Virgo
Symbol: the Virgin
August 23–September 22
Opposite Sign: Virgo

- self-perfection, efficiency, daily routines, reliability, strength of character veiled sensuality, service, hard work, passivity, modesty, incisive communication, shrewd logical thought critical faculties, altruism, honesty, responsibility cleanliness, hygiene, health, healing.

16. You look like a virgin. Are you a Virgo?

17. You seem to have a veiled sensuality. Are you a Virgo?

Libra
Symbol: the Scales
September 23–October 22
Opposite Sign: Aries

- partnership, argument, self-control, good manners, personal appearance refinement, sophistication, good taste, rational thought, ideas for social well being, relationships, ideas, opinions, politics, diplomacy, music, harmony, balance, romance, tact.

18. You look very balanced. Are you a Libra?

19. You look very sophisticated. Are you a Libra?

Scorpio
Symbol: the Scorpion
October 23–November 21
Opposite Sign: Taurus

• metamorphosis, finance, investments, wills, inheritance, hidden matter, secrets, taboos, magic, birth, life, death, sex, sensuality, passion, pushing boundaries of discovery, regeneration, transformation collective unconscious, defense systems, social revolution, reformation, change.

20. You seem to move about like a scorpion. Are you a Scorpio?

21. You seem very passionate. Are you a Scorpio?

22. You seem to be causing a stir. Are you a Scorpio?

Sagittarius
Symbol: the Archer
November 22–December 22
Opposite Sign: Gemini

• spiritual growth, optimism, positive outlook, forward planning, travel, freedom of movement, the outdoors, honesty, justice, morality, imagination, aspirations, philosophy, idealism, religion, open-mindedness, wit, intellect, flashes of intuition, generosity, pleasure, romance.

23. You seem to have look of being well traveled. Are you a Sagittarius?

24. You seem romantic. Are you a Sagittarius?

Capricorn
Symbol: the Goat
December 22–January 19
Opposite Sign: Cancer

- success, high status, good quality, reputation, responsibility, difficulties, problems, paternalism, practicality, realism, hard work, accomplishment, planning, determination, persistence, authority, discipline, money, wealth, long-term projects, wisdom, loyalty, sensitivity to beauty.

25. You move around like a goat. Are you a Capricorn?

26. You seem successful. Are you a Capricorn?

Aquarius
Symbol: the Water Carrier
January 20–February 18
Opposite Sign: Leo

- friendship, courtesy, kindness, tranquillity, mystery, intrigues, magic, genius, originality, eccentricity, independence, humanitarian issues, fame, recognition, politics, creative arts, electricity, magnetism, telecommunication, scientific analysis, experimentation, detachment.

27. The symbol for Aquarius is the water carrier and I see you are carrying a beer. Are you an Aquarius?

28. You seem to have a genius to your ways. Are you an Aquarius?

Bonus Chapter
Using Color to Pick Up Women

Color is an underused weapon in the pursuit of women. Not only do colors have understood meanings in our cultures but they also have a subconscious effect on us.

There are two ways that you can use colors in your pick-up strategy. First, you can select your clothes on a color interpretation basis. For instance you can wear all black if you are looking to convey a persona of power and sophistication. On the flip side if you want to be seen as warm and vibrant you can wear a shirt that is bright red. The choice is up to you.

The other way you can use color in your pick-up strategy is to observe the colors of your targeted lady's clothing and make a comment based on it. Using this strategy shows that you are an observant and intelligent suitor and these are qualities that any woman will admire. So take a look at the universal interpretation of the colors below—including red, pink, orange, yellow, green, blue, purple, brown, grey, and black—and use them at your will. Go get them!

Red is associated with excitement, drama, urgent passion, strength, and assertiveness. It is also know to be an appetite stimulant.

1. (To a girl wearing red): They say the color red is an appetite stimulant. Are you trying to make guys hungry for you?

2. (To a girl wearing red): Are you as passionate as your shirt?

3. (To a girl wearing red): You know with a little white and blue you would be a great representative for the United States.

Pink is associated with girls. Pinks are considered the warmest and most cheerful of colors. Soft pinks have been known to generate simple, uncomplicated emotions.

4. (To a girl wearing pink): Well, who's this beautiful flower?

5. (To a girl wearing pink): What do you think of men who wear pink?

Orange has associations with fire, vitality, warmth, and energy.

6. (To a girl wearing orange): Do you wear orange because you are juicy?

7. (To a girl wearing orange): Are you full of positive warm energy like your shirt?

Yellow is associated with warmth, the sun, warning, caution, happiness, cheerfulness, expansiveness, and lack of inhibition.

8. (To a girl wearing yellow): Is your yellow meant for guys to slow down or speed up when they walk past you?

9. (To a girl wearing yellow): Do you worship the sun?

Green is associated with nature, growth, optimism, good luck, freshness, fertility, finance, business, economic stability, and entitlement.

10. (To a girl wearing green): With that green on are you trying to say that you have money or you're looking for money?

11. (To a girl wearing green): They say green represents both fertility and greed. Which one do you associate with more?

Blue has associations with power, authority, confidence, a sense of safety, trust-worthiness, and peacefulness.

2. (To a girl wearing blue): Do you know karate or anything because the color blue is associated with safety and protection?

3. (To a girl wearing blue): I see you're wearing blue, which is associated with peace. Do you smoke weed?

Purple is associated with the mystic, magic, sensitive intimacy, union, enchant-ment, and the blurring of thought, desire, and reality.

4. (To a girl wearing purple): Purple is often associated with intimacy and union and that's exactly what I'm looking for.

5. (To a girl wearing purple): Purple is often associated with magic. Can you put a love spell on yourself to make you fall in love with me?

Brown is associated with hearth, home, and family security.

6. (To a girl wearing brown): Are you a momma's girl because brown is associated with the home?

7. (To a girl wearing brown): Are you a hippie because brown is often associated with Mother Earth?

Gray communicates an element of non-involvement or concealment. It's a color that remains uncommitted and uninvolved.

8. (To a girl wearing grey): You know grey is the color of concealment. Are you trying to conceal your love for me?

9. (To a girl wearing grey): You know grey is the color of concealment. Are you trying to conceal your phone number from me?

Black is associated with prestige, power, renunciation, surrender and relinquish-ment. The classic tuxedo is black, along with the limousine. One who wears all black is looking to command authority and respect.

10. (To a girl wearing black): How was the funeral?

11. (To a girl wearing black): Do you like dark men too or just clothes?

Epilogue

Well I hope that you enjoyed *Pick-Up Lines That Work: Get the Girl Tonight!* It is my hope that you will use the knowledge contained within the book to make your life with women everything you want it to be.

Please visit www.winningwithgirls.com to learn more techniques in picking up women and to let me know how you enjoyed the book. If you have a success story with using the book please send me an email at success@ winningwithgirls.com.

Good Luck,

Devon "Mack" Wild

0-595-32368-5

CPSIA information can be obtained
at www.ICGtesting.com
Printed in the USA
FSOW01n0823040117
29203FS

9 780595 323685